Harvard Business Review

ON

STRATEGIC SALES

MANAGEMENT

THE HARVARD BUSINESS REVIEW PAPERBACK SERIES

The series is designed to bring today's managers and professionals the fundamental information they need to stay competitive in a fast-moving world. From the preeminent thinkers whose work has defined an entire field to the rising stars who will redefine the way we think about business, here are the leading minds and landmark ideas that have established the *Harvard Business Review* as required reading for ambitious businesspeople in organizations around the globe.

Other books in the series:

Other books in the series (continued):

Harvard Business Review

ON

STRATEGIC SALES MANAGEMENT

A HARVARD BUSINESS REVIEW PAPERBACK

The *Harvard Business Review* articles in this collection are available as
individual reprints. Discounts apply to quantity purchases. For information and ordering, please contact Customer Service, Harvard Business
School Publishing, Boston, MA 02163. Telephone: (617) 783-7500 or
(800) 988-0886, 8 A.M. to 6 P.M. Eastern Time, Monday through Friday.
Fax: (617) 783-7555, 24 hours a day. E-mail: custserv@hbsp.harvard.edu.

Library of Congress Cataloging-in-Publication Data
Harvard business review on strategic sales management.
      p.   cm. — (The Harvard business review paperback series)
  Based on the July-August 2006 special issue of the Harvard
business review.
    Includes index.
    ISBN-13: 978-1-4221-1492-6 (pbk. : alk. paper)
    ISBN-10: 1-4221-1492-9
    1. Sales management.   I. Harvard business review.
HF5438.4.H374 2007
658.8′1—dc22   2007004364

Contents

Harvard Business Review

ON

STRATEGIC SALES
MANAGEMENT

How Right Should the Customer Be?

ERIN ANDERSON AND VINCENT ONYEMAH

Executive Summary

IF YOUR SALESPEOPLE aren't sure who their boss is—the district manager? the regional manager? the customer?— it could be a sign that your company's sales force controls are working at cross-purposes and that your sales function is in trouble.

Sales force controls are the policies and practices that govern the way you train, supervise, motivate, and evaluate your sales staff. They include the types of compensation you offer your people and the criteria your sales managers use to evaluate the reps' performance. These controls let salespeople know which trade-offs the company would prefer them to make when the inevitable conflicts arise between what they want to do (spend lots of time and money to get a sale) and what they actually can do (use limited resources and still get the sale).

When sales force controls aren't aligned—when, say, the system simultaneously encourages reps to be entrepreneurial but also to file detailed call reports and check in frequently with their bosses—individuals become discouraged and unproductive, and they eventually leave the company.

The authors' research suggests there are significant differences between the control systems of companies that encourage salespeople to put the customer first—outcome control (OC) systems—and those that encourage reps to put their managers first—behavior control (BC) systems. In this article, they list the characteristics of OC and BC systems, describe the potential fallout from conflicts within these systems, and explain how you can tell which control system is appropriate for your firm. In most cases, the right choice will be a consistent system somewhere in the middle of the OC-BC continuum.

EVERY ONE OF YOUR SALESPEOPLE will tell you that the customer is king. Sometimes, they'll mean it, and that's usually a good thing. If you press them, your salespeople may even tell you that the district or regional manager is king, and that's not necessarily a bad thing either. The problems come when your salespeople aren't quite sure who their boss is. Their confusion could be a sign that your company's sales force controls—the various policies and practices that define the way you manage your sales team—are in conflict with one another. In researching sales and sales force dynamics over two decades, we've found that this misalignment invariably creates problems in sales functions. As salespeople struggle to resolve or work around the conflicts within the system, the consequences mount—first affecting individuals, then spreading to the entire sales force, and eventually hobbling the whole organization. Over time, the sales force begins losing its best people. Turnover rates soar. One European multinational we studied had lost half its salespeople in its home market every year for five years. Even if a company isn't in such obviously dire straits, it may still be leaving a lot of money on the table.

Our statistical study of more than 2,500 salespeople working in 38 countries for 50 companies suggests there are significant, often overlooked, differences between management systems that encourage salespeople to put the customer first and those that encourage sales reps to put their district or regional managers first. In this article, we'll describe the potential fallout from conflicts within your sales force management system, and we'll explain how you can tell which kind of control system is appropriate for your company's strategy, competitive environment, capabilities, and time horizon.

A Tale of Two Cultures

The culture and effectiveness of any sales force are products of its management system: the rules that govern the way a company trains, monitors, supervises, motivates, and evaluates salespeople. The system signals, in a continuous and more-or-less automatic way, what management expects from its sales team. It conveys to salespeople which trade-offs the company would prefer them to make when the inevitable conflicts arise between what they want to do (spend lots of time and money to get a sale) and what they actually can do (utilize limited resources and still get the sale). The system also affects the way sales reps perceive business challenges, how they think and feel about their roles, how they go about their jobs, and what kinds of indicators they focus on.

All sales force management systems have eight basic components. Among these are the degree of management's intervention in daily sales activities, the types of compensation offered to salespeople, and the number and types of criteria managers use to evaluate salespeople's performance. (For a complete list, see "Who's Calling the Shots?" at the end of this article.) The policies and practices that make up each component can be placed somewhere on a continuum between systems that encourage sales reps to put the customer first—what we call outcome control (OC) systems—and those that get them to put the district or regional manager first—what we call behavior control (BC) systems. Companies that rely on OC systems focus on getting salespeople to deliver certain kinds of results and are essentially indifferent to how those results are obtained. By contrast, firms that rely on BC systems value *how* people make sales more than the number of sales they make.

OC SYSTEMS: THE CUSTOMER IS KING

Companies with outcome control systems measure and reward results—the outcomes of sales reps' interactions with customers. These results can take many forms: sales, margins, contributions to profit, share of customer wallet, market share, sales of new products, repeat business, on-time collection of receivables, and so forth. Companies tend to emphasize and track only a few of these results. Firms with OC systems typically tie salespeople's compensation closely to two or three key metrics, and a substantial portion of each salesperson's compensation is determined by customers' behavior.

Salespeople at OC firms enjoy considerable autonomy and are expected to use it. The company sees them as entrepreneurs who craft and execute personal strategies to find and land their customers. The reps place more importance on pleasing their customers than on pleasing their managers. They will always take the customer's side in negotiating with the company because that relationship will always be more important for them. The employer is simply an income-producing entity, and, as a result, salespeople at OC firms are likely to switch to any employer who offers a more promising pay package and better products to sell.

Managers in OC systems are few and stretched thin, often because they are expected to generate their own sales as well as supervise. They often have minimal contact with their salespeople. In fact, they don't really manage their staffs in the traditional sense. Instead, they negotiate with their direct reports, seeking to convince them that what management wants is in the best interests of the sales team.

The culture in OC firms is competitive. When a sales rep makes a big sale, everyone knows it. Rewards are tangible—something the neighbors and mothers-in-law can see. This includes money, of course, but also trips, cars, merchandise, expense account lifestyles, and symbols of recognition such as plaques, trophies, or pictures in the company newsletter. Salespeople in these systems have no qualms about showing off their rewards because they know they may not always have them. If results fall off, they pay the price.

BC SYSTEMS: THE MANAGER IS KING

Companies with BC systems evaluate and reward what salespeople bring to the job. Management measures what salespeople *actually* do—their efforts, activities, hours, expenses, and the like. It measures what salespeople *can* do (theoretically, at least)—their knowledge, skills, competencies, and aptitudes. And it measures what salespeople *are*—their appearance, hygiene, education, age, and so on. Sales managers at BC firms also rely on a plethora of performance criteria, many of them subjective (How attractive is this salesperson?) or difficult to observe (How good are her closing abilities?). Indeed, the evaluation standards are often opaque, and the managers themselves may not be sure just how they apply them. The bulk of compensation in BC companies is fixed (capped salaries), and the variable component is tied to the attitudes, behaviors, and competencies that management prizes.

Because performance evaluations and compensation are inextricably linked in BC systems, sales managers' words of guidance aren't all that different from their explicit directives. Salespeople in BC firms are attentive to any and all management cues. They talk about what the company wants, expects, and rewards—and what it will want, expect, and reward in the future. It's clear that, at some level, somebody is worrying about the numbers. But in the here and now, salespeople focus on, demand, do, and become whatever they think their first-line supervisors will work into their performance evaluations.

While salespeople at BC firms care about tangible, visible acknowledgements, much of their motivation rests on intrinsic rewards such as feelings of achievement, personal growth, and self-worth derived from solving problems, and the satisfaction of offering good service. Factors such as collegiality, training, potential for promotion, and office perks matter to them. And while sales reps in BC systems take the customer's side to some extent, they readily understand that the company must capture its fair share of value.

Of course, the two control systems are at extremes, and many companies function quite well somewhere in the middle, where the power of the manager and the power of the customer are in some sort of balance. Indeed, this is where most sales forces should be. Few firms should be turning over wholesale control of their salespeople to just the customer or just the sales manager.

Maintaining the balance, however, is difficult because people have a natural tendency to work toward the extreme that suits them. Over time, a company's most experienced, successful salespeople will generally push for an outcome control orientation—especially for OC-style compensation. They deliver results, and they know these results will usually trump the sales manager's concerns in the eyes of that manager's own boss. For their part, sales managers have a natural tendency toward empire building and want more obedience from their salespeople, so they will naturally push for a behavior control system. They will probably insist that salespeople involve them more in the selling process, hand in reports on sales calls, and so forth.

Taken singly, each incremental change lobbied for and made will seem reasonable. Collectively, such changes can spell disaster. Empowering salespeople to go get results has its virtues. Likewise, limiting salespeople's autonomy offers advantages. But managers may not see that trying to do both at the same time doesn't work. Eventually, various components of the sales force management system start migrating to different extremes. A company may use many criteria to evaluate its salespeople (BC style) but may also offer minimal or no monitoring and coaching (OC style)—and the system as a whole loses consistency. Because it happens slowly, many organizations are oblivious that their control systems have become misaligned. Salespeople have learned to live with it—or have quit.

Managers have come to accept it and perhaps like it. (See the sidebar "Your Sales Force Is Misaligned—Why Haven't You Noticed?" at the end of this article.) Bringing all the elements of a sales organization back into alignment can be politically and financially difficult. And since firms aren't aware of the results they *could* be getting, they don't realize that their inconsistent control systems are hurting their performance.

Gauging Your Consistency

To get a sense of how consistent your sales management efforts are, it might be useful to render the system graphically. (See the exhibit "How Consistent Is Your Control System?") For each of the system components, plot where your approach to sales force management falls on the outcome control–behavior control continuum. If your system is consistent, the points should fall roughly in a straight line. If your system isn't consistent, you will observe a pronounced zigzag design.

There are three common patterns of inconsistency. The most frequent type of mismatch is characterized by "the ever-present manager." An example of this would be a company that generally uses an outcome control system—managers focus on a handful of important results when evaluating sales reps' performance and calibrate compensation accordingly—but that has interventionist managers (BC style), who have regular contact with salespeople and monitor the reps' activities intensely. Yet for all their interactions, the managers don't coach as much as a true behavior control system calls for. In this system, salespeople will resist management's interference and will try to focus on pay and bottomline sales figures. Meanwhile, managers will try to correct salespeople's "excessive" focus on generating "unprofitable" orders, will complain that salespeople are uncooperative, and will struggle to redirect salespeople's attention to whatever the managers think should be done. We found just this situation at a company selling premium graphic services. Because the firm's clients differed in size and needs, salespeople had to tailor their product pitches to each buyer and occasion. The reps were paid largely on

How Consistent Is Your Control System?

To find out where your company falls on the outcome control–behavior control continuum, consider each of the eight basic system components and indicate which camp you fall in (or closest) to. If you can plot a relatively straight line, your system is well balanced. If the line zigzags, you need to take a closer look at how your sales function works.

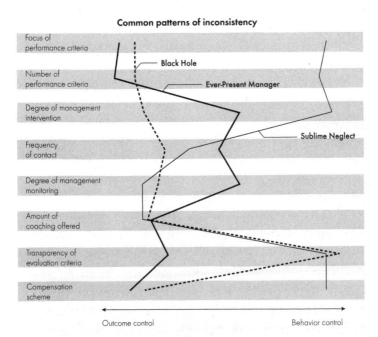

Common patterns of inconsistency

commission and were evaluated on a handful of sales performance indicators, which encouraged them to do whatever they had to in order to make the sale. But they also had to contend with interventionist managers, who worked overtime to find out what the salespeople were doing and would frequently tell them to do something else. The friction this created sapped everyone's energy, to the customers' detriment. Fortunately, the firm's sales managers recognized the problem in time and made an effort to intervene less.

Another common mismatch, "sublime neglect," is characterized by a BC system that doesn't provide salespeople with sufficient coaching from and contact with management. Salespeople don't know what management thinks and how they should behave—and the customer is not empowered to fill the vacuum. At one company we studied, a health management firm, the sales management system's values, metrics, and evaluation were essentially about behavior control. But the managers who were supposed to coach and monitor salespeople were largely absent; they had their own selling responsibilities. So it was difficult for the sales reps to obtain the guidance they needed to work effectively. The company's frequent rotation of sales managers aggravated the problem: The salespeople constantly had to adapt to new and idiosyncratic demands from new chiefs. (Remember: If the boss is king, his whims must be taken seriously.)

The third common type of inconsistent system, "the black hole," is characterized by a fundamentally OC system with opaque evaluation methods. Salespeople feel like the organization is focused only on results; how those results translate into individual performance evaluations (and corresponding pay raises and other rewards) is a mystery. Salespeople in companies with

these characteristics are cynical about a culture they
consider arbitrary and political; high performers become
frustrated and lose motivation. That was the case at a
large bank in West Africa we studied. It employed close
to 4,000 salespeople, who called on individual customers
for deposits. The typical salesperson was a college graduate with little or no banking experience. In theory, a sales
rep's performance was evaluated strictly in terms of the
volume of deposits he or she obtained each month; each
rep had to hit a set target. In practice, however, many
salespeople missed their targets yet kept their jobs. Some
even got promoted ahead of superior performers. The
salespeople sensed that evaluations were based on the
branch manager's whims. The high performers felt
unfairly treated, and many eventually left the company.

Which System Do You Need?

System consistency isn't the whole story. Your straight
line also needs to be in the right place on the outcome
control–behavior control continuum. The location will
depend on your company's situation—the constraints it
faces and the resources, strategy, internal culture, and
time horizon it has. It will also depend on the environment in which you operate. Firms need to bow to local
cultural and legal norms. Outcome control systems are
much better received in some cultures (such as the
United States, Canada, Argentina, Italy, southern Nige-
ria, or parts of India) than in others (such as Sweden,
Japan, or Korea). A firm with global reach, therefore,
should have multiple control systems for its various sales
forces. That said, our study indicates there are general
situations that clearly call for an OC system and others
that require a BC system.

WHEN OUTCOME CONTROL FITS

As a general rule, outcome control fits when your salespeople have a substantial influence on results—that is,
when their skills and efforts are the biggest determinant
of sales. This is equivalent to saying that sales force elas-
ticity is high (changing sales campaigns or salespeople
would have a big effect on results). When sales reps
make that big of a difference to the bottom line, it is
worth it to give them autonomy and to pay them handsomely to do what they do. Specifically, OC is the right
system in the following situations.

Customers Need Information. When customers are
solving a new problem or contemplating new solutions
to existing problems, they need a great deal of information. They don't know what they don't know, but they
realize their decisions have high stakes. Such customers
will take their time, gather information, and process it.
In this situation, a good salesperson slowly and invisibly
frames the customer's thinking—and an OC system will
ensure that the rep is putting forth his or her best effort.

The Sale Is Open. In some companies, certain sales
transactions have an air of predictability or presale
momentum. The firm with the biggest advertising budget or the lowest price usually takes a commanding lead
over its rivals. But in many sales situations, it's hard to
forecast who will win. That's when a good salesperson
can sway decisions. As in the need-for-information sce-
nario, an OC system can inspire salespeople to work their
hardest and think more creatively.

Customers Trust the Salesperson. In some industries, customers can forge strong ties to a salesperson

and will buy whatever he or she recommends. For instance, customers will let a great salesperson from an investment services firm frame their thinking. They trust "their" financial adviser. Such advisers are more likely to be working in an OC system than in a BC system.

There Are Many Ways to Close the Deal. An OC system works when you know that many different behaviors can be effective in generating results. In that case, why impose management's favorites? OC also fits when you don't know which behaviors work and which don't. For instance, the insurance industry relies heavily on OC systems because it is dealing with both classic customer interactions (constant, cyclical demand for products like life insurance and car insurance) as well as niche sales situations (insurance plans for people with certain preexisting health conditions).

The OC firm must permit its salespeople to be independent, which can be difficult. One of us ran a meeting of sales managers in a would-be OC firm. For 20 minutes, it proved impossible to get down to business. Why? The managers wanted to complain about how disrespectfully their subordinates treated them. The comments from one salesperson about a manager's ugly ties were bad enough, the managers said. But when one sales rep reminded everyone in a meeting that the top sales performer that year had earned more than the manager? Well, that was outrageous, the managers said. In truth, real OC firms wouldn't consider such behavior outrageous. They would celebrate it—even if the top salesperson made more money than the CEO.

Many companies are like the one we advised: They try to keep the paychecks in line with the hierarchy. This is dangerous. If management in an OC system announces caps on income—or worse, imposes them after a sales campaign is under way—it will cost that company more in the long run than it will save. If your internal culture cannot accept that someone who is "just a salesperson" might be autonomous and wealthy (just like an entrepreneur), OC is not for you. This is a major reason why OC firms are less common in many national cultures, such as France and Germany, both of which place great importance on hierarchy.

Finally, for an OC system to work properly, you need an excellent accounting system. It should be timely (you can't wait too long to pay people), accurate (you don't want to have to reissue paychecks), and appropriate (reflecting who is selling what to whom). Many firms simply cannot measure outputs well enough by themselves to operate an OC system; they have to invest in information systems that can do the work for them. An express-delivery firm we worked with spent millions to reconfigure its IT system, which could only track packages from warehouses to recipients. The new system tracks packages from senders—right down to the individual who made the delivery request—and links the information back to the salesperson who then targets that individual. Similarly, drug companies work with third parties, such as IMS Health (a provider of market intelligence to the health care industry), to collect information on filled prescriptions from pharmacies. The drug companies then match the data to individual physicians (in the United States) or to physician groups (in Europe) and, further, to the salespeople who call on these doctors and medical groups.

WHEN BEHAVIOR CONTROL FITS

In general, you need a BC system when your salespeople can't figure out what to do with their autonomy. Otherwise, customers' demands will drive your salespeople to errors that will rebound to your detriment. Specifically, BC systems are a good match in the following scenarios.

Your Salespeople Lack Experience. It takes both savoir faire (know how to do) and savoir être (know how to be) to master sales in the field. Without these aptitudes, inexperienced salespeople will flounder and take shortcuts, even some unethical ones. If they manage to survive at the company, they will retain the suboptimal habits that got them where they are. This is a major reason why the insurance industry is under regulatory pressure in many countries. Because of the field's reliance on outcome control and the inexperience of many sales teams due to high turnover, many sales reps are selling the wrong products to the wrong people. Government demands for compliance are really calls for behavior control in an industry habituated to outcome control. Switching to a BC system, however, is not a complete solution. Junior salespeople who will initially thrive under a behavior control system will chafe as they gain experience. That's why many insurance companies run two sales forces in parallel—one OC, and one BC. Salespeople are funneled into the OC system only after they have proven themselves in the BC system. Interestingly, firms that have utilized these twin tracks have discovered that many salespeople never really want to leave the BC system and that many of the salespeople in the OC system voluntarily switch back to BC. By running parallel systems, firms can accommodate their sales reps' changing needs without losing talented, experienced people.

You Need to Protect Your Brand. Many companies have a legitimate need to control how salespeople present their products or services. Your firm may have, or may be trying to build, high brand equity. Or it may be selling a product or a service that is dangerous if it's used incorrectly. In either case, it is critical for your salespeople to present your product or service in excruciatingly correct detail. Misrepresentation, either by omission or commission, is unacceptable. This may be partly why pharmaceutical and chemical industries rely on BC systems to manage their sales forces.

You Have High Nonsales Priorities. Behavior control is the right choice when you want your salespeople to set high nonsales priorities, such as participating in new product development. While such efforts contribute indirectly to current sales and directly to future sales, an OC system—with its focus on the here and now—will encourage salespeople to neglect them. In general, the more you want your salespeople to act like your marketing or strategy people, the more you need to tweak their job descriptions, alleviating for them the burden of closing sales to create their paychecks. Behavior control systems are also better for firms that want to develop leaders and managers. Indeed, that's why we often see OC firms poaching people from BC firms: The OC companies don't have the right kind of system to grow good sales managers.

It's Hard to Assign Sales Credit. BC systems impose fewer demands on accounting than OC systems do, and many firms use behavior controls simply because their sales records don't tell them how much each individual contributes, which makes it difficult to find a workable variable-pay formula. In situations like this, managers can avert endless disputes with their sales staffs by using behavior controls. In some cases, the problem is not so much that a good pay package can't be designed; it's that no one can agree on what the appropriate drivers are.

People often find it easier to adapt to behavior control systems than to outcome control systems. That's because BC systems conform to people's natural instincts to create hierarchies—but they require far more overhead. Behavior control not only imposes salaries on salespeople but also requires a large number of powerful managers who, in turn, need a sensitive, thorough information system that tracks salespeople, their territories, and their competition. Without such a system, managers can't craft effective sales strategies and measure their results. BC only works when you know which behaviors to ask for and which behaviors to discourage.

Ultimately, managing a sales force comes down to helping your salespeople align their priorities with the company's. The best sales force management system—customer is king, manager is king, or some balance of the two—is the one that fits your selling process, time horizon, mission, culture, and information systems. Weigh all the elements pulling you left (OC) or right (BC). In most cases, the best choice will be a consistent system that's somewhere in the middle.

Who's Calling the Shots?

THE POLICIES AND PRACTICES that make up a sales force control system can be categorized into eight components. These reflect the key questions senior management needs to ask about the way it conducts its sales business. How management answers can help determine whether it employs an outcome control system, a behavior control system, or some combination of the two.

System Component	Customers call the shots: Outcome Control	Managers call the shots: Behavior Control
1. Focus of performance criteria. Does management value how sales results are achieved (the effort expended) or simply the results themselves (the outcomes)?	Managers pay particular attention to bottom-line results.	Managers pay particular attention to the methods used to achieve outcomes.
2. Number of performance criteria. Does management judge salespeople using only two or three factors, or does it look at a dozen or more metrics?	Management evaluates a salesperson's performance according to a few observable metrics, primarily those controlled by the customer.	Management evaluates a salesperson's performance subjectively, using many criteria.
3. Degree of management intervention. Who makes the final decision on important issues related to sales assignments, the salesperson or the manager?	Managers offer relatively little supervision. Salespeople make final decisions.	Managers offer relatively heavy supervision and make final decisions.
4. Frequency of contact. Are interactions between salespeople and management easy to enact?	Managers and salespeople have little to no contact.	Managers and salespeople are frequently and extensively in contact.

System Component	Customers call the shots: Outcome Control	Managers call the shots: Behavior Control
5. Degree of management monitoring. Does management show serious interest in salespeople's call and activity reports, or are these just a bureaucratic requirement?	Management rarely monitors its sales staff.	Management constantly monitors its sales staff.
6. Amount of coaching offered. Does management suggest ways that salespeople can improve their selling skills and abilities?	Managers offer little to no coaching.	Managers offer frequent, heavy coaching.
7. Transparency of evaluation criteria. How objective, clear, and precise are evaluations at the company?	Evaluation criteria are very transparent.	Evaluation criteria are opaque.
8. Compensation scheme. Is the paycheck based largely on variable compensation triggered by outcomes? Or does it have a large salary component with a performance bonus driven by management's judgments?	A salesperson's compensation is mostly variable, keyed to customer-generated results.	A salesperson's compensation is mostly fixed, keyed to salary and management's evaluations.

Your Sales Force Is Misaligned— Why Haven't You Noticed?

ON THE SURFACE, inconsistent control systems can seem quite stable. That's because there are always people who not only survive but actually thrive in the inconsistent environment. These individuals' work experiences and sales results give them enough sense to use those parts of the system that work for them and ignore the components that don't. These people, over time, develop coping mechanisms and find opportunities in the contradictions in the system. Such salespeople aren't always homegrown; they may have honed their coping skills elsewhere. But what they may lack in political capital at the company, they make up for with some other asset—a deep Rolodex, for instance, or an industrywide reputation.

If a sales force has a lot of these people, and as long as they perform well enough to offset the nonperformers, an inconsistent control system can seem fine for quite a long time before the defects become apparent. It's usually not a sustainable situation, though. The stars will eventually retire, and as they approach retirement, they will slow down. Meanwhile, it's unlikely that the company will be able to hold on to enough of its most promising newcomers to replace the productivity of the senior salespeople. And recruiting the right kind of outsiders in any quantity will be impossible. When the situation does start to unravel, it will happen fast.

What Price Are You Paying?

IN MANY INDUSTRIES, a salesperson must call on a prospect at least four times to get that first order. The sales rep's efforts after the fifth call boost sales dramatically, but, eventually, the orders taper off. At that point, any extra effort the salesperson expends has little, if any, payoff. A smart (or well-managed) rep instead turns his attention to another goal. Each time the salesperson eyes a new target and investigates ways to approach the threshold for that target, he needs to muster his resources (time, energy, attention, and so on).

Here is where inconsistent control systems do their greatest harm: They send the message that too many things need the sales rep's attention. Lacking a sense of priorities, the salesperson dissipates her resources trying to meet too many goals. She does some of everything because everything is important. In the end, she never passes the threshold performance in whatever goal she's pursuing. Yet she's still expending resources, making investments that won't offer returns. After all, customers don't give salespeople partial credit for their good intentions and fragmented efforts.

In an inconsistent system, salespeople feel like there is no overall logic, no unified direction, to their efforts. They get worn down and worn out. For instance, a salesperson, in an attempt to cover every base, might decide to play it safe and respond to every signal that emanates from management. Suppose that she were expected to make lots of sales calls and write detailed reports on each. She probably wouldn't be able to make enough calls to generate the sales expected of her, and she wouldn't be able to write very informative reports because she couldn't spend enough time per call. If she decided to respond to only some of management's cues, she would run the risk of choosing the wrong ones to follow.

In an inconsistent environment, morale gradually declines. Because the sales rep can't get a succinct message about what is expected of him, he experiences a gnawing sense of "I don't know how I'm doing, let alone what I'm doing." He is consumed by the feeling that there is no way to satisfy all the players—the company, the district manager, the customer. He becomes frustrated and unmotivated, which may lead to his withdrawal and lower performance. Sales managers in inconsistent systems may notice increasing use of unethical practices as their sales reps take shortcuts to deal with conflicting demands. Eventually, this dysfunctional dynamic is reflected in the bottom line: The company's sales expenses creep ahead of the competition's.

Originally published in July–August 2006
Reprint R0607D

Ending the War Between Sales and Marketing

PHILIP KOTLER, NEIL RACKHAM, AND
SUJ KRISHNASWAMY

Executive Summary

SALES DEPARTMENTS TEND to believe that marketers
are out of touch with what's really going on in the
marketplace. Marketing people, in turn, believe the sales
force is myopic—too focused on individual customer
experiences, insufficiently aware of the larger market,
and blind to the future. In short, each group undervalues
the other's contributions. Both stumble (and organizational performance suffers) when they are out of sync.
Yet few firms seem to make serious overtures toward
analyzing and enhancing the relationship between these
two critical functions.

Curious about the misalignment between Sales and
Marketing, the authors interviewed pairs of chief marketing officers and sales vice presidents to capture their perspectives. They looked in depth at the relationship
between Sales and Marketing in a variety of companies

in different industries. Their goal was to identify best practices that could enhance the joint performance and increase the contributions of these two functions. Among their findings:

- The marketing function takes different forms in different companies at different product life cycle stages. Marketing's increasing influence in each phase of an organization's growth profoundly affects its relationship with Sales.

- The strains between Sales and Marketing fall into two main categories: economic (a single budget is typically divided between Sales and Marketing, and not always evenly) and cultural (the two functions attract very different types of people who achieve success by spending their time in very different ways).

In this article, the authors describe the four types of relationships Sales and Marketing typically exhibit. They provide a diagnostic to help readers assess their companies' level of integration, and they offer recommendations for more closely aligning the two functions.

PRODUCT DESIGNERS LEARNED years ago that they'd save time and money if they consulted with their colleagues in manufacturing rather than just throwing new designs over the wall. The two functions realized it wasn't enough to just coexist—not when they could work together to create value for the company and for customers. You'd think that marketing and sales teams, whose work is also deeply interconnected, would have discovered something similar. As a rule, though, they're separate functions within an organization, and, when they do work together, they don't always get along. When sales are disappointing, Marketing blames the sales force for its poor execution of an otherwise brilliant rollout plan. The sales team, in turn, claims that Marketing sets prices too high and uses too much of the budget, which instead should go toward hiring more salespeople or paying the sales reps higher commissions. More broadly, sales departments tend to believe that marketers are out of touch with what's really going on with customers. Marketing believes the sales force is myopic—too focused on individual customer experiences, insufficiently aware of the larger market, and blind to the future. In short, each group often undervalues the other's contributions.

This lack of alignment ends up hurting corporate performance. Time and again, during research and consulting assignments, we've seen both groups stumble (and the organization suffer) because they were out of sync. Conversely, there is no question that, when Sales and Marketing work well together, companies see substantial improvement on important performance metrics: Sales cycles are shorter, market-entry costs go down, and the cost of sales is lower. That's what happened when IBM integrated its sales and marketing groups to create a new function called Channel Enablement. Before the groups were integrated, IBM senior executives Anil Menon and Dan Pelino told us, Sales and Marketing operated independent of one another. Salespeople worried only about fulfilling product demand, not creating it. Marketers failed to link advertising dollars spent to actual sales made, so Sales obviously couldn't see the value of marketing efforts. And, because the groups were poorly coordinated, Marketing's new product announcements often came at a time when Sales was not prepared to capitalize on them.

Curious about this kind of disconnect between Sales and Marketing, we conducted a study to identify best practices that could help enhance the joint performance and overall contributions of these two functions. We interviewed pairs of chief marketing officers and sales vice presidents to capture their perspectives. We looked in depth at the relationship between Sales and Marketing in a heavy equipment company, a materials company, a financial services firm, a medical systems company, an energy company, an insurance company, two high-tech electronic products companies, and an airline. Among our findings:

- The marketing function takes different forms in different companies at different product life-cycle stages—all of which can deeply affect the relationship between Sales and Marketing.

- The strains between Sales and Marketing fall into two main categories: economic and cultural.

- It's not difficult for companies to assess the quality of the working relationship between Sales and Marketing. (This article includes a diagnostic tool for doing so.)

- Companies can take practical steps to move the two functions into a more productive relationship, once they've established where the groups are starting from.

Different Roles for Marketing

Before we look closely at the relationship between the two groups, we need to recognize that the nature of the marketing function varies significantly from company to company.

Most small businesses (and most businesses *are* small) don't establish a formal marketing group at all. Their marketing ideas come from managers, the sales force, or an advertising agency. Such businesses equate marketing with selling; they don't conceive of marketing as a broader way to position their firms.

Eventually, successful small businesses add a marketing person (or persons) to help relieve the sales force of some chores. These new staff members conduct research to calibrate the size of the market, choose the best markets and channels, and determine potential buyers' motives and influences. They work with outside agencies on advertising and promotions. They develop collateral materials to help the sales force attract customers and close sales. And, finally, they use direct mail, telemarketing, and trade shows to find and qualify leads for the sales force. Both Sales and Marketing see the marketing group as an adjunct to the sales force at this stage, and the relationship between the functions is usually positive.

As companies become larger and more successful, executives recognize that there is more to marketing than setting the four P's: product, pricing, place, and promotion. They determine that effective marketing calls for people skilled in segmentation, targeting, and positioning. Once companies hire marketers with those skills, Marketing becomes an independent player. It also starts to compete with Sales for funding. While the sales mission has not changed, the marketing mission has. Disagreements arise. Each function takes on tasks it believes the other should be doing but isn't. All too often, organizations find that they have a marketing function inside Sales, and a sales function inside Marketing. At this stage, the salespeople wish that the marketers would worry about future opportunities (long-term strategy) and leave the current opportunities (individual and group sales) to them.

Once the marketing group tackles higher-level tasks like segmentation, it starts to work more closely with other departments, particularly Strategic Planning, Product Development, Finance, and Manufacturing. The company starts to think in terms of developing brands rather than products, and brand managers become powerful players in the organization. The marketing group is no longer a humble ancillary to the sales department. It sets its sights much higher: The marketers believe it's essential to transform the organization into a "marketing-led" company. As they introduce this rhetoric, others in the firm—including the sales group—question whether the marketers have the competencies, experience, and understanding to lead the organization.

While Marketing increases its influence within separate business units, it rarely becomes a major force at the corporate level. There are exceptions: Citigroup, Coca-Cola, General Electric, IBM, and Microsoft each have a marketing head at the corporate level. And Marketing is more apt to drive company strategy in major packaged-goods companies such as General Mills, Kraft, and Procter & Gamble. Even then, though, during economic downturns, Marketing is more closely questioned—and its workforce more likely to be cut—than Sales.

Why Can't They Just Get Along?

There are two sources of friction between Sales and Marketing. One is economic, and the other is cultural. The economic friction is generated by the need to divide the total budget granted by senior management to support Sales and Marketing. In fact, the sales force is apt to criticize how Marketing spends money on three of the four

P's—pricing, promotion, and product. Take pricing. The marketing group is under pressure to achieve revenue goals and wants the sales force to "sell the price" as opposed to "selling through price." The salespeople usually favor lower prices because they can sell the product more easily and because low prices give them more room to negotiate. In addition, there are organizational tensions around pricing decisions. While Marketing is responsible for setting suggested retail or list prices and establishing promotional pricing, Sales has the final say over transactional pricing. When special low pricing is required, Marketing frequently has no input. The vice president of sales goes directly to the CFO. This does not make the marketing group happy.

Promotion costs, too, are a source of friction. The marketing group needs to spend money to generate customers' awareness of, interest in, preference for, and desire for a product. But the sales force often views the large sums spent on promotion—particularly on television advertising—as a waste of money. The VP of sales tends to think that this money would be better spent increasing the size and quality of the sales force.

When marketers help set the other P, the product being launched, salespeople often complain that it lacks the features, style, or quality their customers want. That's because the sales group's worldview is shaped by the needs of its individual customers. The marketing team, however, is concerned about releasing products whose features have broad appeal.

The budget for both groups also reflects which department wields more power within the organization, a significant factor. CEOs tend to favor the sales group when setting budgets. One chief executive told us, "Why should I invest in more marketing when I can get better results by hiring more salespeople?" CEOs often see sales as more tangible, with more short-run impact. The sales group's contributions to the bottom line are also easier to judge than the marketers' contributions.

The cultural conflict between Sales and Marketing is, if anything, even more entrenched than the economic conflict. This is true in part because the two functions attract different types of people who spend their time in very different ways. Marketers, who until recently had more formal education than salespeople, are highly analytical, data oriented, and project focused. They're all about building competitive advantage for the future. They judge their projects' performance with a cold eye, and they're ruthless with a failed initiative. However, that performance focus doesn't always look like action to their colleagues in Sales because it all happens behind a desk rather than out in the field. Salespeople, in contrast, spend their time talking to existing and potential customers. They're skilled relationship builders; they're not only savvy about customers' willingness to buy but also attuned to which product features will fly and which will die. They want to keep moving. They're used to rejection, and it doesn't depress them. They live for closing a sale. It's hardly surprising that these two groups of people find it difficult to work well together.

If the organization doesn't align incentives carefully, the two groups also run into conflicts about seemingly simple things—for instance, which products to focus on selling. Salespeople may push products with lower margins that satisfy quota goals, while Marketing wants them to sell products with higher profit margins and more promising futures. More broadly speaking, the two groups' performance is judged very differently. Salespeople make a living by closing sales, full stop. It's easy to see who (and what) is successful—almost immediately. But the marketing budget is devoted to programs, not people, and it takes much longer to know whether a program has helped to create long-term competitive advantage for the organization.

Four Types of Relationships

Given the potential economic and cultural conflicts, one would expect some strains to develop between the two groups. And, indeed, some level of dysfunction usually does exist, even in cases where the heads of Sales and Marketing are friendly. The sales and marketing departments in the companies we studied exhibit four types of relationships. The relationships change as the companies' marketing and sales functions mature—the groups move from being unaligned (and often conflicted) to being fully integrated (and usually conflict-free)—though we've seen only a few cases where the two functions are fully integrated.

UNDEFINED

When the relationship is undefined, Sales and Marketing have grown independently; each is preoccupied largely with its own tasks and agendas. Each group doesn't know much about what the other is up to—until a conflict arises. Meetings between the two, which are ad hoc, are likely to be devoted to conflict resolution rather than proactive cooperation.

DEFINED

In a defined relationship, the two groups set up processes—and rules—to prevent disputes. There's a "good fences make good neighbors" orientation; the marketers and salespeople know who is supposed to do what, and they stick to their own tasks for the most part. The groups start to build a common language in potentially contentious areas, such as "How do we define a lead?" Meetings become more reflective; people raise questions like "What do we expect of one another?" The groups work together on large events like customer conferences and trade shows.

ALIGNED

When Sales and Marketing are aligned, clear boundaries between the two exist, but they're flexible. The groups engage in joint planning and training. The sales group understands and uses marketing terminology such as "value proposition" and "brand image." Marketers confer with salespeople on important accounts. They play a role in transactional, or commodity, sales as well.

INTEGRATED

When Sales and Marketing are fully integrated, boundaries become blurred. Both groups redesign the relationship to share structures, systems, and rewards. Marketing—and to a lesser degree Sales—begins to focus on strategic, forward-thinking types of tasks (market sensing, for instance) and sometimes splits into upstream and downstream groups. Marketers are deeply embedded in the management of key accounts. The two groups develop and implement shared metrics. Budgeting becomes more flexible and less contentious. A "rise or fall together" culture develops.

We designed an assessment tool that can help organizations gauge the relationship between their sales and marketing departments. (See the insert "How Well Do Sales and Marketing Work Together?" at the end of this article.) We originally developed this instrument to help us understand what we were seeing in our research, but the executives we were studying quickly appropriated it for their own use. Without an objective tool of this kind, it's very difficult for managers to judge their cultures and their working environments.

Moving Up

Once an organization understands the nature of the relationship between its marketing and sales groups, senior managers may wish to create a stronger alignment between the two. (It's not always necessary, however. The exhibit "Do We Need to Be More Aligned?" can help organizations decide whether to make a change.)

MOVING FROM UNDEFINED TO DEFINED

If the business unit or company is small, members of Sales and Marketing may enjoy good, informal relationships that needn't be disturbed. This is especially true if Marketing's role is primarily to support the sales force. However, senior managers should intervene if conflicts arise regularly. As we noted earlier, this generally happens because the groups are competing for scarce resources and because their respective roles haven't been clearly defined. At this stage, managers need to create clear rules of engagement, including handoff points for important tasks like following up on sales leads.

Do We Need to Be More Aligned?

The nature of relations between Sales and Marketing in your organization can run the gamut—from undefined (the groups act independent of one another) to integrated (the groups share structures, systems, and rewards). Not every company will want to—or should—move from being undefined to being defined or from being defined to being aligned. The following table can help you decide under which circumstances your company should more tightly integrate its sales and marketing functions.

	Undefined	Defined	Aligned
Don't make any changes if . . .	The company is small. The company has good informal relationships. Marketing is still a sales support function.	The company's products and services are fairly cut-and-dried. Traditional marketing and sales roles work in this market. There's no clear and compelling reason to change.	The company lacks a culture of shared responsibility. Sales and Marketing report separately. The sales cycle is fairly short.

Tighten the relationship between Sales and Marketing if . . .

Conflicts are evident between the two functions.

There's duplication of effort between the functions; or tasks are falling through the cracks.

The functions compete for resources or funding.

Even with careful definition of roles, there's duplication of effort between the functions; or tasks are falling through the cracks.

The market is commoditized and makes a traditional sales force costly.

Products are developed, prototyped, or extensively customized during the sales process.

Product life cycles are shortening, and technology turnover is accelerating.

A common process or business funnel can be created for managing and measuring revenue-generating activities.

move to Defined →

move to Aligned →

move to Integrated →

MOVING FROM DEFINED TO ALIGNED

The defined state can be comfortable for both parties. "It may not be perfect," one VP of sales told us, "but it's a whole lot better than it was." Staying at this level won't work, though, if your industry is changing in significant ways. If the market is becoming commoditized, for example, a traditional sales force may become costly. Or if the market is moving toward customization, the sales force will need to upgrade its skills. The heads of Sales and Marketing may want to build a more aligned relationship and jointly add new skills. To move from a defined relationship to an aligned one:

Encourage Disciplined Communication. When it comes to improving relations between any two functions, the first step inevitably involves improving communication. But it's not as simple as just *increasing* communication between two groups. More communication is expensive. It eats up time, and it prolongs decision making. We advocate instead for more *disciplined* communication. Hold regular meetings between Sales and Marketing (at least quarterly, perhaps bimonthly or monthly). Make sure that major opportunities, as well as any problems, are on the agenda. Focus the discussions on action items that will resolve problems, and perhaps even create opportunities, by the next meeting. Salespeople and marketers need to know *when* and *with whom* they should communicate. Companies should develop systematic processes and guidelines such as, "You should involve the brand manager whenever the sales opportunity is above $2 million," or "We will not go to print on any marketing collateral until salespeople have reviewed it," or "Marketing will be invited to the top ten critical account reviews." Businesses also need to establish an up-to-date, user-friendly "who to call" database. People get frustrated—and they waste time—searching in the wrong places for help.

Create Joint Assignments; Rotate Jobs. As your functions become better aligned, it's important to create opportunities for marketers and salespeople to work together. This will make them more familiar with each other's ways of thinking and acting. It's useful for marketers, particularly brand managers and researchers, to occasionally go along on sales calls. They should get involved with developing alternate solutions for customers, early in the sales process. And they should also sit in on important account-planning sessions. Salespeople, in turn, should help to develop marketing plans and should sit in on product-planning reviews. They should preview ad and sales-promotion campaigns. They should share their deep knowledge about customers' purchasing habits. Jointly, marketers and salespeople should generate a playbook for expanding business with the top ten accounts in each market segment. They should also plan events and conferences together.

Appoint a Liaison from Marketing to Work with the Sales Force. The liaison needs to be someone both groups trust. He or she helps to resolve conflicts and shares with each group the tacit knowledge from the other group. It's important not to micromanage the liaison's activities. One of the Marketing respondents in our study described the liaison's role this way: "This is a person who lives with the sales force. He goes to the staff meetings, he goes to the client meetings, and he goes to the client strategy meetings. He doesn't develop product;

he comes back and says, 'Here's what this market needs. Here's what's emerging,' and then he works hand in hand with the salesperson and the key customer to develop products."

Colocate Marketers and Salespeople. It's an old and simple truth that when people are physically close, they will interact more often and are more likely to work well together. One bank we studied located its sales and marketing functions in an empty shopping mall: Different groups and teams within Sales and Marketing were each allocated a storefront. Particularly in the early stages of moving functions toward a more closely aligned relationship, this kind of proximity is a big advantage. Most companies, though, centralize their marketing function, while the members of their sales group remain geographically dispersed. Such organizations need to work harder to facilitate communication between Sales and Marketing and to create shared work.

Improve Sales Force Feedback. Marketers commonly complain that salespeople are too busy to share their experiences, ideas, and insights. Indeed, very few salespeople have an incentive to spend their precious time sharing customer information with Marketing. They have quotas to reach, after all, and limited time in which to meet and sell to customers. To more closely align Sales and Marketing, senior managers need to ensure that the sales force's experience can be tapped with a minimum of disruption. For instance, Marketing can ask the Sales VP to summarize any sales force insights for the month or the quarter. Or Marketing can design shorter information forms, review call reports and CRM data independently, or pay salespeople to make themselves available to interviewers from the marketing group and to summarize what their sales colleagues are thinking about.

MOVING FROM ALIGNED TO INTEGRATED

Most organizations will function well when Sales and Marketing are aligned. This is especially true if the sales cycle is relatively short, the sales process is fairly straightforward, and the company doesn't have a strong culture of shared responsibility. In complicated or quickly changing situations, there are good reasons to move Sales and Marketing into an integrated relationship. (The exhibit "Sales and Marketing Integration Checklist" outlines the issues you'll want to think through.) This means integrating such straightforward activities as planning, target setting, customer assessment, and value-proposition development. It's tougher, though, to integrate the two groups' processes and systems; these must be replaced with common processes, metrics, and reward systems. Organizations need to develop shared databases, as well as mechanisms for continuous improvement. Hardest of all is changing the culture to support integration. The best examples of integration we found were in companies that already emphasized shared responsibility and disciplined planning; that were metrics driven; that tied rewards to results; and that were managed through systems and processes. To move from an aligned relationship to an integrated one:

Appoint a Chief Revenue (or Customer) Officer. The main rationale for integrating Sales and Marketing is that the two functions have a common goal: the generation of

Sales and Marketing Integration Checklist

To achieve integration between Sales and Marketing, your company needs to focus on the following tasks.

Integrate Activities	Integrate Processes and Systems	Enable the Culture	Integrate Organizational Structures
☐ Jointly involve Sales and Marketing in product planning and in setting sales targets.	☐ Implement systems to track and manage Sales and Marketing's joint activities.	☐ Emphasize shared responsibility for results between the different divisions of the organization.	☐ Split Marketing into upstream and downstream teams.
☐ Jointly involve Sales and Marketing in generating value propositions for different market segments.	☐ Utilize and regularly update shared databases.	☐ Emphasize metrics.	☐ Hire a chief revenue officer.
☐ Jointly involve Sales and Marketing in assessing customer needs.	☐ Establish common metrics for evaluating the overall success of Sales and Marketing efforts.	☐ Tie the rewards to results.	
☐ Jointly involve Sales and Marketing in signing off on advertising materials.	☐ Create reward systems to laud successful efforts by Sales and Marketing.	☐ Enforce divisions' conformity to systems and processes.	
☐ Jointly involve Sales and Marketing in analyzing the top opportunities by segment.	☐ Mandate that teams from Sales and Marketing meet periodically to review and improve relations.		
	☐ Require Sales and Marketing heads to attend each other's budget reviews with the CEO.		

profitable and increasing revenue. It is logical to put both functions under one C-level executive. Companies such as Campbell's Soup, Coca-Cola, and FedEx have a chief revenue officer (CRO) who is responsible for planning for and delivering the revenue needed to meet corporate objectives. The CRO needs control over the forces affecting revenue—specifically, marketing, sales, service, and pricing. This manager could also be called the chief customer officer (CCO), a title used in such companies as Kellogg; Sears, Roebuck; and United Air Lines. The CCO may be more of a customer ombudsman or customer advocate in some companies; but the title can also signal an executive's broader responsibility for revenue management.

Define the Steps in the Marketing and Sales Funnels. Sales and Marketing are responsible for a sequence of activities and events (sometimes called a funnel) that leads customers toward purchases and, hopefully, ongoing relationships. Such funnels can be described from the customer's perspective or from the seller's perspective. (A typical funnel based on the customer's decision sequence is shown in the exhibit "The Buying Funnel.") Marketing is usually responsible for the first few steps—building customers' brand awareness and brand preference, creating a marketing plan, and generating leads for sales. Then Sales executes the marketing plan and follows up on leads. This division of labor has merit. It is simple, and it prevents Marketing from getting too involved in individual sales opportunities at the expense of more strategic activities. But the handoff brings serious penalties. If things do not go well, Sales can say that the plan was weak, and Marketing can say that the salespeople did not work hard enough or smart enough. And in companies where Marketing

The Buying Funnel

There's a conventional view that Marketing should take responsibility for the first four steps of the typical buying funnel—customer awareness, brand awareness, brand consideration, and brand preference. (The funnel reflects the ways that Marketing and Sales influence customers' purchasing decisions.) Marketing builds brand preference, creates a marketing plan, and generates leads for sales before handing off execution and follow-up tasks to Sales. This division of labor keeps Marketing focused on strategic activities and prevents the group from intruding in individual sales opportunities. But if things do not go well, the blame game begins. Sales criticizes the plan for the brand, and Marketing accuses Sales of not working hard enough or smart enough.

The Sales group is responsible for the last four steps of the funnel—purchase intention, purchase, customer loyalty, and customer advocacy. Sales usually develops its own funnel for the selling tasks that happen during the first two steps. (These include prospecting, defining needs, preparing and presenting proposals, negotiating contracts, and implementing the sale.) Apart from some lead generation in the prospecting stage, Marketing all too often plays no role in these tasks.

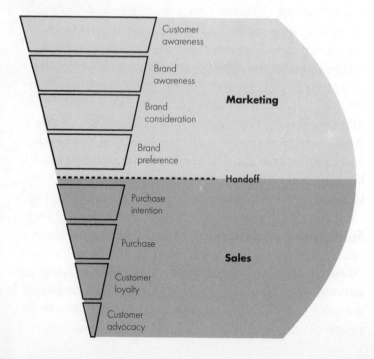

makes a handoff, marketers can lose touch with active customers. Meanwhile, Sales usually develops its own funnel describing the sequence of selling tasks. Funnels of this kind—integrated into the CRM system and into sales forecasting and account-review processes—form an increasingly important backbone for sales management. Unfortunately, Marketing often plays no role in these processes. Some companies in our study, however, have integrated Marketing into the sales funnel. During prospecting and qualifying, for instance, Marketing helps Sales to create common standards for leads and opportunities. During the needs-definition stage, Marketing helps Sales develop value propositions. In the solution-development phase, Marketing provides "solution collateral"—organized templates and customizing guides so salespeople can develop solutions for customers without constantly having to reinvent the wheel. When customers are nearing a decision, Marketing contributes case study material, success stories, and site visits to help address customers' concerns. And during contract negotiations, Marketing advises the sales team on planning and pricing. Of course, Marketing's involvement in the sales funnel should be matched by Sales' involvement in the upstream, strategic decisions the marketing group is making. Salespeople should work with the marketing and R&D staffs as they decide how to segment the market, which products to offer to which segments, and how to position those products.

Split Marketing into Two Groups.   There's a strong case for splitting Marketing into upstream (strategic) and downstream (tactical) groups. Downstream marketers develop advertising and promotion campaigns, collateral material, case histories, and sales tools. They help salespeople develop and qualify leads. The downstream team uses market research and feedback from the sales reps to help sell existing products in new market segments, to create new messages, and to design better sales tools. Upstream marketers engage in customer sensing. That is, they monitor the voice of the customer and develop a long view of the company's business opportunities and threats. The upstream team shares its insights with senior managers and product developers—and it participates in product development.

Set Shared Revenue Targets and Reward Systems. The integrated organization will not succeed unless Sales and Marketing share responsibility for revenue objectives. One marketing manager told us, "I'm going to use whatever tools I need to make sure Sales is effective, because, at the end of the day, I'm judged on that sales target as well." One of the barriers to shared objectives, however, is the thorny issue of shared rewards. Sales-people historically work on commission, and marketers don't. To successfully integrate the two functions, management will need to review the overall compensation policy.

Integrate Sales and Marketing Metrics. The need for common metrics becomes critical as Marketing becomes more embedded in the sales process and as Sales plays a more active role in Marketing. "In order to be the customer-intimate company we are," says Larry Norman, president of Financial Markets Group, part of the Aegon USA operating companies, "we need to be metrics driven and have metrics in place that track both sales and marketing performance." On a macro level, companies like General Electric have "the number"—the sales goal to which both Sales and Marketing commit. There is no escaping the fact that, however well integrated Sales and Marketing are, the company will also want to develop metrics to measure and reward each group appropriately.

Sales metrics are easier to define and track. Some of the most common measures are percent of sales quota achieved, number of new customers, number of sales closings, average gross profit per customer, and sales expense to total sales. When downstream marketers become embedded in the sales process—for example, as members of critical account teams—it's only logical to measure and reward their performance using sales metrics. But then how should the company evaluate its upstream marketers? On the basis of the accuracy of their product forecasting, or the number of new market segments they discover? The metrics will vary according to the type of marketing job. Senior managers need to establish different measures for brand managers, market researchers, marketing information systems managers, advertising managers, sales promotion managers, market segment managers, and product managers. It's easier to construct a set of metrics if the marketers' purposes and tasks are clearly outlined. Still, given that upstream marketers are more engaged in sowing the seeds for a better future than in helping to reap the current harvest, the metrics used to judge their performance necessarily become softer and more judgmental.

Obviously, the difference between judging current and future outcomes makes it more complicated for companies to develop common metrics for Sales and Marketing. Upstream marketers in particular need to be assessed according to what they deliver over a longer period. Salespeople, meanwhile, are in the business of converting potential demand into today's sales. As the working relationship between Sales and Marketing becomes more interactive and interdependent, the integrated organization will continue to wrestle with this difficult, but surely not insurmountable, problem.

SENIOR MANAGERS OFTEN DESCRIBE the working relationship between Sales and Marketing as unsatisfactory. The two functions, they say, undercommunicate, underperform, and overcomplain. Not every company will want to—or should—upgrade from defined to aligned relationships or from aligned to integrated relationships. But every company can and should improve the relationship between Sales and Marketing. Carefully planned enhancements will bring salespeople's intimate knowledge of your customers into the company's core. These improvements will also help you build better products for the future. They will help your company marry softer, relationship-building skills with harder, analytic skills. They will force your organization to closely consider how it rewards people and whether those reward systems apply fairly across functions. Best of all, these improvements will boost both your top-line and bottom-line growth.

How Well Do Sales and Marketing Work Together?

THIS INSTRUMENT IS INTENDED to help you gauge how well your sales and marketing groups are aligned and integrated. Ask your heads of Sales and Marketing (as well as their staffs) to evaluate each of the following statements on a scale of 1 to 5, where 1 is "strongly disagree" and 5 is "strongly agree." Tally the numbers, and use the scoring key to determine the kind of relationship Sales and Marketing have in your company. The higher the score, the more integrated the relationship. (Several companies have found that their sales forces and their marketing staffs have significantly different perceptions about how well they work together—which in itself is quite interesting.)

1. Our sales figures are usually close to the sales forecast. _____

2. If things go wrong, or results are disappointing, neither function points fingers or blames the other. _____

3. Marketing people often meet with key customers during the sales process. _____

4. Marketing solicits participation from Sales in drafting the marketing plan. _____

5. Our salespeople believe the collateral supplied by Marketing is a valuable tool to help them get more sales. _____

6. The sales force willingly cooperates in supplying feedback requested by Marketing. _____

7. There is a great deal of common language here between Sales and Marketing. _____

8. The heads of Sales and Marketing regularly confer about upstream issues such as idea generation, market sensing, and product development strategy. _____

9. Sales and Marketing work closely together to define segment buying behavior. _____

10. When Sales and Marketing meet, they do not need to spend much time on dispute resolution and crisis management. _____

11. The heads of Sales and Marketing work together on business planning for products and services that will not be launched for two or more years. _____

12. We discuss and use common metrics for determining the success of Sales and Marketing. _____

13. Marketing actively participates in defining and executing the sales strategy for individual key accounts. _____

14. Sales and Marketing manage their activities using jointly developed business funnels, processes, or pipelines that span the business chain—from initial market sensing to customer service. _____

Key: 1= Strongly Disagree; 2 = Disagree; 3 = Neither; 4 = Agree; 5 = Strongly Agree

15. Marketing makes a significant contribution to analyzing data from the sales funnel and using those data to improve the predictability and effectiveness of the funnel.   _____

16. Sales and Marketing share a strong "We rise or fall together" culture.   _____

17. Sales and Marketing report to a single chief customer officer, chief revenue officer, or equivalent C-level executive.   _____

18. There's significant interchange of people between Sales and Marketing.   _____

19. Sales and Marketing jointly develop and deploy training programs, events, and learning opportunities for their respective staffs.   _____

20. Sales and Marketing actively participate in the preparation and presentation of each other's plans to top executives.   _____

Total _____

Scoring
20-39 Undefined   60-79 Aligned
40-59 Defined   80-100 Integrated

Key: 1= Strongly Disagree; 2 = Disagree; 3 = Neither; 4 = Agree; 5 = Strongly Agree

Originally published in July–August 2006
Reprint R0607E

Match Your Sales Force Structure to Your Business Life Cycle

ANDRIS A. ZOLTNERS, PRABHAKANT SINHA,
AND SALLY E. LORIMER

Executive Summary

ALTHOUGH COMPANIES DEVOTE considerable time
and money to managing their sales forces, few focus
much thought on how the structure of the sales force
needs to change over the life cycle of a product or a
business. However, the organization and goals of a
sales operation have to evolve as businesses start up,
grow, mature, and decline if a company wants to keep
winning the race for customers.

Specifically, firms must consider and alter four factors
over time: the differing roles that internal salespeople
and external selling partners should play, the size of the
sales force, its degree of specialization, and how salespeople apportion their efforts among different customers,
products, and activities. These variables are critical
because they determine how quickly sales forces

respond to market opportunities, they influence sales reps' performance, and they affect companies' revenues, costs, and profitability.

In this article, the authors use time-series data and cases to explain how, at each stage, firms can best tackle the relevant issues and get the most out of their sales forces. During start-up, smart companies focus on how big their sales staff should be and on whether they can depend upon selling partners. In the growth phase, they concentrate on getting the sales force's degree of specialization and size right. When businesses hit maturity, companies should better allocate existing resources and hire more general-purpose salespeople. Finally, as organizations go into decline, wise sales leaders reduce sales force size and use partners to keep the business afloat for as long as possible.

SMART BICYCLE-RACING TEAMS match their strategies to the stages of a race in order to win. In the flat stretches, team members take turns riding in front because it's easier for the team leader to pedal when someone ahead is cutting the wind. In the mountains, some riders make the task easier for the leader by setting the pace and by choosing the best line of ascent. In the time trials, a few team members maintain steady speeds over long distances to lower the team's average finishing time. Talent always matters, but in most races, the way teams deploy talent over time, in different formations in different contexts, makes the difference between winning and losing.

That's a lesson sales leaders must learn. Although companies devote considerable time and money to managing their sales forces, few focus much thought on how the sales force needs to change over the life cycle of a product or a business. However, shifts in the sales force's structure are essential if a company wants to keep winning the race for customers. Specifically, companies must alter four factors over time: the roles that the sales force and selling partners play; the size of the sales force; the sales force's degree of specialization; and how salespeople apportion their efforts among different customers, products, and activities. These variables are critical because they determine how quickly sales forces respond to market opportunities; they influence sales forces' performance; and they affect companies' revenues, costs, and profitability.

Admittedly, it isn't easy for a company to change the composition and activities of its sales force. Salespeople and customers resist change, often quite fiercely. If a company starts hiring specialists instead of general-purpose salespeople, for example, or reassigns accounts from sales reps in the field to telesales staff, existing salespeople will have to learn how to sell different products and will have to terminate some customer relationships. If they earn commissions or bonuses, their income may fall in the short run. Customers, too, will have to adjust to new processes and establish relationships with new salespeople. As a result, businesses tend to change their sales structures only when major events—such as the failure to meet targets, a change in rivals' strategies, or mergers—force them to do so.

This conservatism doesn't serve companies well. The sales force structure that works during start-up is different from what works when the business is growing, during its maturity, and through its decline. The four life-cycle phases aren't mutually exclusive; some companies display characteristics of more than one stage at the same time. Many businesses go through the four stages in turn, but when new technologies or markets emerge, companies can also move nonsequentially through the life cycle stages. These days, businesses tend to go through the four phases more quickly than they used to, which makes it even more important to have a flexible sales force.

Over the past 25 years, we and our colleagues at ZS Associates have studied the sales force structures of approximately 2,500 businesses in 68 countries. Our research shows that companies that change their sales force structures in ways that correspond loosely to the stages a product or business goes through in its life cycle are more successful than those that don't.

During start-up, smart companies focus on whether they should depend on selling partners or create their own sales forces. If they decide to set up sales organizations, they pay a lot of attention to sizing them correctly. As companies grow, sizing issues become even more important. In addition, executives must decide when to invest in specialist sales forces. When businesses hit maturity, the emphasis shifts to making sales forces more effective by appointing account managers and better allocating salespeople's resources, and making them more cost-efficient by using less expensive people such as telesales staff and sales assistants. Finally, as organizations go into decline, sales leaders' attention shifts to reducing the size of sales forces and using even more cost-efficient ways to cover markets. In the following pages, we'll explore in depth how companies can develop the best sales force structures for each of the four stages of the business life cycle. (See the exhibit "The Four Factors for a Successful Sales Force.")

The Four Factors for a Successful Sales Force

A company must focus on different aspects of its sales force structure over the life cycle of the business, just as it matches customer strategy to the life cycle of a product.

	Business Life Cycle State			
	Start-Up	Growth	Maturity *Emphasis*	Decline
Role of sales force and selling partners	★★★★	★★	★	★★★
Size of sales force	★★★	★★★★	★★	★★★★
Degree of specialization	★	★★★★	★★★	★★
Sales force resource allocation	★★	★	★★★★	★
Underlying customer strategy	Create awareness and generate quick product uptake	Penetrate deeper into existing segments and develop new ones	Focus on efficiently serving and retaining existing customers	Emphasize efficiency, protect critical customer relationships, exit unprofitable segments

Start-Up: Making the Right Moves Early

Sales leaders of new companies and new divisions of existing companies are eager to exploit opportunities in the marketplace and are under pressure to demonstrate success quickly. While a start-up has to worry constantly about selling costs, a new division can draw on some of the parent company's financial and human resources. Still, since both their sales forces must create awareness about new products and generate quick sales, the organizations face the same structural dilemmas.

DO IT YOURSELF, OR OUTSOURCE?

The central decision that a new business must make is whether it should sell its products directly to customers or sell them through partners. Although many entrepreneurs outsource the sales function, that may not always be the right decision.

To be sure, by tying up with other companies, new ventures save the costs of building and maintaining sales forces. Partnerships can also help executives manage risk better since start-ups often pay only commissions on sales; if products don't sell, their costs are minimal. Moreover, new businesses can enter markets rapidly by working alongside companies that have sales expertise, influence over sales channels, and relationships with potential customers. For example, in the 1990s, Siebel Systems used systems integration consultants, such as Accenture, to build its enterprise software business quickly.

Companies that decide to outsource the sales function should segment the market and develop sales processes that meet each segment's needs. Then they should select a partner, or partners, that will implement those selling processes effectively. To succeed, a company needs its selling partners' attention. Start-ups must develop partner management systems that include marketing programs and incentive schemes and appoint partner managers who provide selling partners with encouragement, process assistance, sales analytics, and end-user data. All too frequently, companies rely on money to motivate partners, not realizing that incentives aren't a substitute for systems and supervision. Companies should track performance closely, quickly terminate agreements with partners that don't perform well, and shift to selling directly when it's in their long-term interest to do so.

In our experience, many businesses depend on their selling partners for too long. When companies outsource the sales function, they don't control the selling activity, have little power over salespeople, gain no channel power, and don't own customer relationships. As time goes by, it becomes more, not less, difficult to reduce dependence on selling partners. Many firms become stuck in partnerships that inhibit growth. Take the case of SonoSite. When it launched the world's first handheld ultrasound machine in 1999, the company decided to use a well-known distributor to sell the product in the United States. Since the ultrasound device was technologically complex, the distributor needed to educate potential customers. That required a multistep selling process, which the distributor didn't use for the other products it sold. After two years of disappointing sales, SonoSite dropped the distributor and started selling the device itself. A year after it had staffed its sales force fully, its revenues rose by 79%.

Although outsourcing is popular today, we're convinced that companies should use selling partners only if they stand to gain strategic advantages as well as cost benefits. Those advantages come in several flavors. Many partners turn products into solutions, which can greatly increase sales. For example, value-added resellers create systems that combine their own software with computer hardware from different manufacturers. Start-ups also gain access to customers when their products become part of an assortment that a partner offers. For instance, a computer accessories manufacturer could benefit by tying up with distributor CDW, which delivers a range of computer-related equipment to companies in the United States. Only when partners provide strategic advantages are selling relationships likely to endure.

HOW BIG SHOULD THE SALES STAFF BE?

During the start-up phase, sales forces have to educate potential customers about products and change customers' buying processes before they can generate sales. Salespeople also must chase down and make every possible sale in order to drive business. That's a lot of work, but new ventures have limited capital to invest in attracting and developing good salespeople. As a result, many new businesses adopt an "earn your way" approach to sizing their sales forces—they start small and add more feet on the street after they have generated the money to pay for them.

This approach sounds eminently logical but often results in companies leaving money on the table (see the exhibit "How Sales Sizing Strategies Stack Up"). Between 1998 and 2004, we forecast the sales and profit implications of different sales force sizes for 11 start-ups in the health care industry. In ten of the companies, sales leaders chose to create teams that were smaller than the optimal size. In fact, the average size was just 64% of the

How Sales Sizing Strategies Stack Up

In their infancy, companies often undersize sales forces. The charts show the impact of three different sizing scenarios on one pharmaceutical company's profits. The figures are projections based on mathematical models. The pharmaceutical company, which started with 300 salespeople, found that an "earn your way" approach to staffing (increasing the sales force only as fast as revenues increase) resulted in the highest first-year contribution, but it yielded the lowest three-year contribution. The longer-term contribution was highest with a "quick build" strategy (quickly ramping up the size of the sales force to the long-term optimal level).

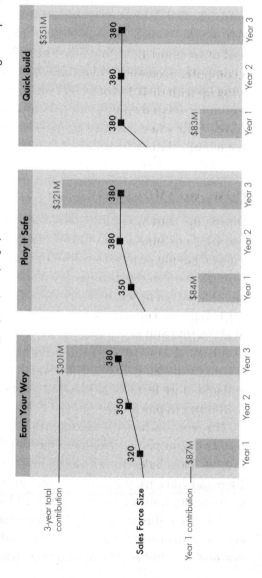

optimal. By not hiring enough salespeople, each of those companies missed the opportunity to earn tens of millions of dollars in additional sales and profits in their first three years. Tellingly, only one business sized its sales force optimally during the start-up stage—and it went on to become the leader in an overcrowded market segment.

We don't fault sales leaders for investing cautiously when they are short of cash or if the future is uncertain. The trouble is, most companies don't increase their investments in sales forces even when the future becomes clear. The moment signs of success emerge, businesses should increase the size of their sales forces quickly and aggressively. Otherwise, they will forfeit sales and profits—and, perhaps, even their futures.

On the flip side, start-up divisions of existing companies often overinvest in salespeople. Their desire to be competitive results in sales forces that, given the nature of the business opportunity, are too big to be profitable.

Growth: Building on Success

During the start-up stage, many companies' product lines are narrow, and they operate in a small number of markets. As businesses grow, their product portfolios expand, and their sales forces have to call on prospects in a broader set of markets. This presents sales managers with two challenges: specialization and size.

THE NEED TO SPECIALIZE

In the growth phase, it's not sufficient for many companies to maintain a sales force of generalists who sell the entire product line to all markets. Salespeople need to master multiple products, markets, and selling tasks at this stage. As repeat sales become a larger proportion of sales, customers will require service and support, adding to salespeople's workloads. As tasks grow beyond the salespeople's capacity to perform their jobs, they are likely to drop the customers, products, and selling activities that are most difficult to manage. Unfortunately, what they drop may be lucrative or strategic opportunities for the business. At this point, companies need to set up specialist sales forces.

Some specialist sales teams focus on products, others on markets, and still others on customer segments. Sales forces can also specialize in certain activities: Some salespeople concentrate on acquiring customers and others on servicing existing customers. Every kind of specialization has benefits and costs. For instance, specialization by markets reduces salespeople's focus on products, while product or activity specialization forces customers to deal with multiple salespeople. Many companies therefore create hybrid structures that include a mix of generalists as well as market, product, and activity specialists. One well-known software company has hired account managers to focus on all the needs of its major customers. The company's product specialists call on midsize clients that don't generate enough business to warrant account managers, and its generalist salespeople cover small companies whose needs don't justify visits by several product specialists.

The transition from a multipurpose sales force to a specialized one is always tough. The work changes considerably, and customer relationships are disrupted. Sales forces may need to adopt team-based selling techniques, making coordination and collaboration vital. The people who succeed in a team-based setting are likely to be different from the lone wolves who do well in a traditional sales force. Consequently, companies may have to recast parts of their sales forces.

Rejuvenated businesses face a slightly different predicament. When a company goes back into growth gear after a period of maturity or decline, its new offerings will have different value propositions and will open up new markets. Salespeople will need to sell differently, and they'll need retraining to do so. Companies may consider splitting their sales forces into groups that specialize in selling old and new products. If neither education nor restructuring delivers results, the company may have to replace the sales force.

Companies must revisit sizing issues when they move from generalist sales forces to specialist ones. On the one hand, specialists will have to cover larger distances than generalists did in order to call on the same number of customers; this means they'll lose time in travel. The company will therefore need more of them to cover its customer base. On the other hand, specialists are more effective than generalists are, so each sales call will be more profitable.

GETTING THE SIZE RIGHT

Growth is usually a happy time in the evolution of a sales force. Sales come in relatively easily, and salespeople are full of optimism. Even so, companies often make critical errors in sizing their sales forces. They continue to understaff, and as a result, they're unable to capitalize on all the opportunities that exist.

Most companies invest conservatively in salespeople because they don't realize that increasing the size of the sales force has short-term and long-term consequences.

When new salespeople come on board, they initially generate small revenue increases. As time goes by, their impact gets bigger. That happens for several reasons. First, new salespeople are not as effective as they will be when they become veterans. Second, in markets with long selling cycles, it takes months of effort before salespeople clinch sales. Third, many purchases, especially in business markets, are not onetime orders but multiyear contracts. Finally, carryover sales—sales that accrue in the future but are the result of sales efforts in the present—vary across products and markets, but they represent a significant portion of every company's long-term revenues.

When a company increases the size of its sales force, it doesn't maximize sales or profits at first. Over time, however, the company will make more profits than if it had started with a smaller sales force. We analyzed data from sizing studies that ZS Associates conducted between 1998 and 2001 for 50 companies. We found that the sales force size that maximizes companies' three-year profits is 18% larger, on average, than the size that maximizes one-year profits. Such findings create competing priorities for sales leaders, who want long-term success but feel pressure to meet annual profit targets. Besides, they rightly believe that three-year projections are less accurate than one-year forecasts. A cautious approach is justified if there is considerable uncertainty over the future, but most sales leaders favor cost-minimizing tactics over profit-maximizing ones, even when the likelihood of success is high. Consequently, they don't hire enough salespeople to exploit the market fully.

Behavioral influences, too, exert pressure on executives to keep sales forces small. Most salespeople resist giving up accounts. They argue that new sales territories aren't justified; some threaten to join competitors if management reduces their accounts bases. For instance, in 2005, when an American medical devices company set out to add 25 sales territories, salespeople and sales managers resisted. They exerted so much pressure that the company eventually created only 12 new territories, which resulted in lower sales and profits than the business could have generated by hiring more salespeople.

Sales leaders can reduce this kind of resistance by fostering a culture of change. They must set expectations early, so that salespeople realize from the outset that, as the business grows, there will be changes in territories and compensation. Some companies periodically reassign accounts between territories to maintain the right balance. Others set lower commission rates on repeat sales, or pay commissions, after the first year, only after a salesperson's revenues exceed a certain level. These tactics give companies the flexibility to expand territories and sales forces in the future.

A company should determine the most appropriate size for its sales force by evaluating the probable size of the opportunity and assessing the potential risks of pursuing an aggressive or conservative approach. An aggressive strategy is appropriate when the business has a high likelihood of success and management has confidence in the sales projections. A more conservative strategy works when greater uncertainty surrounds the business's success.

Two types of sizing errors are common. First, if sales force growth is aggressive, but the market opportunity is moderate, the company will end up having to reduce its sales force. Second, if sales force growth is conservative, but the market opportunity is large, a business may forfeit its best chance to become a market leader. To make better decisions about sales force sizing, companies must invest in market research and in developing forecasting methods and sales response analytics. (See "Sizing the Sales Force by the Numbers" at the end of this article.)

Maturity: The Quest for Effectiveness and Efficiency

Eventually, products and services start to lose their advantage, competition intensifies, and margins erode. At this stage, sales leaders must rely more on resourcefulness than on increasing the scale of the sales effort. Their strategy should emphasize retaining customers, serving existing segments, and increasing the efficiency and effectiveness of the sales force.

OPTIMIZING RESOURCES

In the maturity phase, companies must focus on optimizing the sales force's effectiveness. A study we conducted in 2001 shows that mature companies boosted their gross margins by 4.5% when they resized their sales forces and allocated resources better. While 29% of those gains came because the companies corrected the size of their sales forces, 71% of the gains were the result of changes in resource utilization.

Companies often don't optimize the allocation of their sales resources for several reasons. First, they use the wrong rules. For instance, executives often target customers with the highest potential even though these customers prefer to buy from competitors. Smart companies allocate more resources to products and markets that respond well to salespeople. Second, businesses frequently don't have data on the sales potential of accounts and territories or the responsiveness of potential customers to sales efforts.

There are no shortcuts on the road to effectiveness, though. Organizations can allocate resources best if they measure how responsive different products and markets are to sales efforts. Executives can do that by comparing sales results among similar-sized customers to whom they allotted different levels of effort. That analysis allows a company to evaluate the financial implications of different allocation scenarios. The company can then manage its sales force, even offering incentives on occasion, so that salespeople expend effort in the most productive ways. (See "Optimizing the Maturity Phase" at the end of this article.)

Businesses often find sales effort wasted. Some salespeople try to sell everything in the bag; others spend too much time with familiar or easy-to-sell products. Product managers may dangle the wrong incentives, distracting salespeople from spending time with more profitable offerings. In mathematical terms, a company maximizes long-term profits from its sales force when the incremental return on sales force effort is equal across products. But according to a study ZS Associates conducted in 2001, the ratio of the largest incremental return to the smallest return often runs as high as 8:1. That suggests a serious misallocation of selling effort among products. For instance, one business we studied wanted 100 salespeople to sell 37 products. Each item would have received, on average, just 2.7% of the sales force's time. An analysis revealed that the company's profits would soar if the sales force concentrated on just eight products. In fact, our studies show that focused strategies usually deliver better results than across-the-board ones. Thus, a company makes the greatest profits when its sales force spends its time with the most valuable subset of customers or with the most valuable products in its basket.

Good territorial alignment—the assignment of accounts, prospects, or geographies to salespeople—is a frequently overlooked productivity tool. When businesses adopt unsystematic approaches to carving up territories, sales force effort will not match customer needs. To measure the extent of the problem, in 2000, we analyzed data from 36 territorial alignment studies that we had conducted in eight industries in the United States and Canada. Our analysis showed that 55% of sales territories were either too large or too small. Because of the mismatches, businesses were passing up between 2% and 7% of revenues every year. Companies can create and maintain territorial alignment by measuring the time and effort necessary to service customers every year. They should take accounts away from salespeople who can't give them sufficient attention and transfer the accounts to those who don't have enough work.

THE ACCOUNT MANAGER'S EMERGENCE

Many a business discovers in the maturity stage that the use of product specialists is posing coordination problems and confusing customers that must deal with several salespeople. Smart companies appoint managers for the largest accounts. These account managers coordinate the sales effort and bring in product specialists when customers need expertise. In addition to increasing revenues, the appointment of account managers boosts customer satisfaction and often reduces selling costs.

During an American medical-products company's growth phase in the 1990s, it added a specialist sales force for almost every new product it launched. Eventually, some large hospitals had more than 30 salespeople from the company visiting them every week, many of whom called on the same contacts. Travel costs soared, and, worse, customers became confused by the large number of salespeople visiting them. Realizing the problem, the company reduced the number of specialist salespeople and added managers to coordinate selling activities at large accounts. That helped the company save costs and strengthen customer relationships.

Companies must also find the most inexpensive ways to get work done. They can use sales assistants and part-time salespeople to woo small or geographically dispersed customers and to sell easy-to-understand products. Businesses can also use telesales staff to perform activities that don't require face-to-face contact with customers. For example, one newspaper company we consulted with hired sales assistants in 2005 to take over several nonselling and administrative tasks. Before the assistants arrived, salespeople spent only 35% of their time with prospects and customers. The assistants' arrival freed them to spend more time on sales-related tasks. In addition, since the assistants received lower salaries than the salespeople did, the sales force's efficiency rose sharply.

Decline: Living to Fight Another Day

Companies go into decline when products lose their edge and customers shift to rivals. As CEOs search for breakout strategies, sales forces must do everything they can to help businesses remain viable. The most vital decisions relate, as they did during the start-up stage, to the sales force's size and the role of selling partners, but executives' choices depend on whether or not they foresee a turnaround.

WHEN A TURNAROUND IS LIKELY

Some businesses know their decline is temporary. They plan to boost revenues and profits in the not-too-distant future by launching new products or by merging with other companies. However, turnarounds often demand different sales force structures than the ones companies have. A smart company therefore determines what kind of structure it will need for the sales force to achieve its new goals. Then it identifies and preserves elements of the current structure that are consistent with the one it will need. That's critical; executives shouldn't tear down the parts of the sales organization that will be valuable in the future. For instance, companies often downsize sales forces to save costs in the short run, although they may need more, not fewer, salespeople to implement new strategies.

Many sales leaders take advantage of temporary declines to eliminate mediocrity in their sales forces. Once the turnaround starts, they hire salespeople who are more qualified than the ones they let go. Sometimes what looks like a misallocation of resources is really mediocre performance. Take the case of a Chicago-based software company that was in decline in the 1990s. The company's sales process evolved appropriately, with salespeople becoming skilled at protecting current business. When the firm launched some new products, it realized that few of its salespeople had the skills and appetite to pursue new customers and markets aggressively. Instead of sacking salespeople, the software firm created two roles: current account managers, or "farmers," and new business developers, or "hunters." The veterans continued to manage existing customers, which suited their capabilities, while sales leaders hired most of the new business developers from outside the organization. That helped the software company move quickly from decline to growth.

WHEN A TURNAROUND ISN'T LIKELY

When further decline is inevitable, sales organizations can only ensure that companies remain profitable for as long as possible. Businesses should use their salespeople to service the most profitable, loyal, and strategically important customers, and service other accounts through low-cost selling resources such as telesales staff or external partners.

Protecting the most loyal customers and the best salespeople are top priorities. Companies need to focus loving attention on key customers that, fearing the salespeople managing their accounts will soon be gone, will entertain competitive offerings. They must reassure these critical accounts about the immediate future, particularly by retaining star salespeople. When the sales force starts to worry about downsizing, the best salespeople will be the first to leave. Even as companies prepare to let other people go, they must pay stars handsomely to keep them. In addition, strong leadership is essential during downsizing, and only timely and straightforward communication from sales leaders can maintain a reasonable level of morale and motivation.

To decide how quickly it should reduce head count, a company must assess the market opportunity that remains and the risks of different downsizing strategies. A gradual sales force reduction works well when the opportunity is declining at a modest rate, but it is a poor strategy when the market is disappearing quickly. Errors are common. Many businesses downsize the sales force slowly, remaining hopeful between each wave of layoffs that the trend will reverse. When it doesn't, the high cost of the sales force will render the company unprofitable faster. One common tactic for gradual downsizing is a hiring freeze. That isn't an effective way to downsize sales forces, particularly when the opportunity decline is significant. Sales force attrition usually doesn't occur quickly, and if salespeople who cover important accounts leave, a hiring freeze will result in suboptimal market coverage.

Rapid sales force reduction is the best course when the market is in a steep decline. Survivors will know they have some kind of job security, customers will have greater confidence about what the future holds, and sales leaders can start building a smaller, more focused sales organization. The risk with rapid sales force reduction, though, is that if the decline turns out to be less severe than expected, more people will lose their jobs than necessary. Although the business will remain profitable for a while, the rate of decline will be greater than if head count reductions had been modest. If there's a lot of uncertainty about the rate at which the market is shrinking, companies should consider downsizing the sales force in small but discrete steps.

Improving the efficiency of sales forces and searching for lower-cost selling channels are critical when companies are in decline. By using less-expensive selling resources, companies can continue selling to some segments. That entails moving the coverage of some customers from specialty salespeople to generalists, and shifting the coverage of other customers from field sales-people to telesales staff. As in the maturity stage, companies can shift the selling of easy-to-understand products and the execution of administrative tasks to less expensive resources, such as sales assistants, telesales staff, part-time salespeople, and the Internet.

It's not easy, but a systematic cost-reduction program can help companies live to fight another day. Take the case of an American lubricant manufacturer that in early 2005 needed to cut costs radically to preserve profitability. The company revised its channel strategy, moving the coverage of thousands of customers to selling partners. Those partners had less expensive overheads, such as office space and employee benefits, so their costs were lower than those of the manufacturer. The company shrank its sales force and got the remaining salespeople to focus on selling only to large customers. By the end of the year, the lubricant company had turned the corner.

SALES LEADERS WHO TRY to match sales force structures with the business life cycle face different challenges at every stage. The common thread, though, is that they must overcome organizational resistance at each step and sacrifice short-term profits to secure their companies' success over time.

Sizing the Sales Force by the Numbers

EVERY COMPANY IN GROWTH MODE should conduct a break-even analysis to check if its sales force is the right size. That involves computing the break-even ratio (the ratio of the incremental sales revenue per additional salesperson to the break-even sales), estimating the carryover sales rates, and using those estimates to determine the three-year return on investment in sales staff.

To determine the break-even ratio:

1. Estimate the annual cost of a salesperson (**C**), the gross margin (**M**), which is the amount of sales revenue that the business keeps as profit after deducting variable costs, and the gross margin rate (**M_R**) which is gross margin expressed as a percentage of sales revenue.

2. Calculate break-even sales by dividing the cost of a salesperson by the gross margin rate. ($C \div M_R = B$). That's the amount a salesperson must sell in a year to cover his or her costs.

3. Estimate the incremental sales revenue that an additional salesperson could generate in a year (**I**).

4. Divide the incremental sales revenue per additional salesperson by the break-even sales to compute the break-even ratio (**$I \div B$**). A ratio of 2.00, for instance, implies that a new salesperson will generate gross margin equal to twice his or her cost in a year.

Break-even =

To determine the carryover sales percentage:

5. Estimate the percentage, based on past trends, of this year's sales that the company will retain in future years without any sales force effort. Those are the carryover sales percentages (**K_2** for next year and **K_3** for the year after).

To determine the three-year ROI on sales staff:

6. Take the sum of the gross margin on the incremental sales revenue that an additional salesperson can generate in year 1, the incremental gross margin on carryover sales in year 2, and the incremental gross margin on carryover sales in year 3.

7. Subtract from that sum the annual cost of an additional salesperson.

8. Divide the total by the additional salesperson's annual cost. The result is expressed as a percentage. The formula looks like this:

$$[(M_R \times I) + (M_R \times I \times K_2) + (M_R \times I \times K_3) - C] \div C$$

The break-even ratio and the first-year carryover rate can tell you how to size your sales force. In the table below, the numbers in each cell represent three-year returns on sales force investment. Businesses can set their own criteria, but in our experience, companies have sized their sales forces optimally when the ROI is between 50% and 150%. If the ROI is below 50%, the sales force is too large, and if it is over 150%, the force is too small.

New salesperson sales/ break-even sales	Carryover									
	0%	10%	20%	30%	40%	50%	60%	70%	80%	90%
0.25	-75%	-72%	-69%	-65%	-61%	-56%	-51%	-45%	-39%	-32%
0.50	-50%	-45%	-38%	-31%	-22%	-13%	-2%	10%	22%	36%
0.75	-25%	-17%	-7%	4%	17%	31%	47%	64%	83%	103%
1.00	0%	11%	24%	39%	56%	75%	96%	119%	144%	171%
1.25	25%	39%	55%	74%	95%	119%	145%	174%	205%	239%
1.50	50%	67%	86%	109%	134%	163%	194%	229%	266%	307%
1.75	75%	94%	117%	143%	173%	206%	243%	283%	327%	374%
2.00	100%	122%	148%	178%	212%	250%	292%	338%	388%	442%
2.25	125%	150%	179%	213%	251%	294%	341%	393%	449%	510%
2.50	150%	178%	210%	248%	290%	338%	390%	448%	510%	578%
2.75	175%	205%	241%	282%	329%	381%	439%	502%	571%	645%
3.00	200%	233%	272%	317%	368%	425%	488%	557%	632%	713%
3.25	225%	261%	303%	352%	407%	469%	537%	612%	693%	781%
3.50	250%	289%	334%	387%	446%	513%	586%	667%	754%	849%
3.75	275%	316%	365%	421%	485%	556%	635%	721%	815%	916%
4.00	300%	344%	396%	456%	524%	600%	684%	776%	876%	984%

Oversized   Right size   Undersized

Optimizing the Maturity Phase

Mature companies optimize their resources when sales forces focus on the customers, products, and selling activities that generate the highest response to their sales efforts. To do that, sales leaders must ask themselves the following questions:

Resource Allocation Decisions

Customer

What market segments should we focus on:

- High volume or low volume?
- Highly profitable or less profitable?
- National accounts or smaller accounts?
- New or old accounts?

What industries do we call on?
What geographic areas do we focus on: local, regional, national, or international? Which accounts should headquarters staff call on, and which should field sales call on?

Product

What products should we focus on:

- Existing or new?
- High volume or relatively low volume?
- Easy to sell or hard to sell?
- Familiar or unfamiliar?
- Differentiated or nondifferentiated?

- Products with long selling cycles or short selling cycles?

- Products with high short-term impact and low carryover or with low short-term impact and high carryover?

Activity
What activities should we focus on:

- Hunting for new customers or retaining old customers?

- Selling or servicing?

  How do we allocate relationship experts, product experts, and industry experts?

Originally published in July–August 2006
Reprint R0607F

Understanding What Your Sales Manager Is Up Against

BARRY TRAILER AND JIM DICKIE

Executive Summary

EVERY YEAR, the research firm CSO Insights publishes the results of its Sales Performance Optimization survey, an online questionnaire given to more than 1,000 sales executives worldwide that seeks to examine the effectiveness of key sales practices and metrics. In this article, two partners from CSO provide the 2005 and 2006 survey highlights, which describe the challenges today's sales organizations face and how they're responding.

An overall theme is the degree to which the buy cycle has gotten out of sync with the sell cycle. Buyers have always had a buy cycle, starting at the point they perceive a need. Sellers have always had a sales cycle, starting at the point they spot a prospect. Traditionally, the two have dovetailed—either because the seller created the buyer's perception of need or because the buyer pursued a need by contacting a salesperson (often for product information). Now the buy cycle is often well under way before the seller is even aware there is a cycle—in part because of the information asymmetry created by the Internet. The implications for managing a sales organization are profound in that sales training must now address how reps handle an environment in which buyers have more knowledge than they do.

The authors offer evidence that sales executives are taking—and should take—aggressive action to train and retain sales talent, manage the sales process, and use sales support technologies to meet the challenges of this new environment.

F OR THE PAST 12 YEARS, we have conducted an annual survey of chief sales officers—the executives in charge of their companies' selling efforts. One purpose is to understand what challenges their sales organizations are up against and how those challenges are shifting over time. The 1,275 responses to our 2006 survey indicate an acceleration of trends established over the past several years. Across industries, the selling context has changed, buyers are behaving differently, and the work required of the sales organization is becoming more difficult.

Let's start with the fact that 85% of companies report increases in their product-line breadth, product com-plexity, *and* participation in new markets. The impact on the sales organization comes in many forms. It takes longer to get a new salesperson up to full productivity: 62% of companies report a ramp-up period of more than seven months. The percentage has risen in each of the past four years, but it made its most dramatic one-year jump from 2005 to 2006. The quotas being assigned to salespeople have also gone up substantially. While this is to be expected, given the rebound in the world's major economies, we were surprised at the level of change—an almost 20% increase, on average, from 2005 to 2006. Meanwhile, sales reps have less help in meeting their goals. The ratios of sales support personnel to sales reps and of sales managers to sales reps both widened.

Somehow, even with such higher demands, quota attainment has not suffered—58% of reps made their quotas in 2005, and 59% in 2006. But various conversion metrics suggest this increased production is the result of just that much more hard work. For example, the past several years have seen declines in the percentages of leads resulting in initial meetings, initial meetings leading to formal presentations, and presentations resulting in sales. The past year alone saw a 5% to 8% decline in these metrics—a big step backward in productivity. (See the exhibit "More Work, Less to Show for It.")

These figures are symptomatic of the more than 100 sales-performance metrics we asked about. Not every metric shows deterioration, but it's hard to imagine anyone concluding from our data that sales has become an easier job.

Diverging Cycles

In-depth interviews with sales executives help to clarify why the data are trending as they are. In the broadest sense, it's because the buyer's cycle has become decoupled from the seller's. Buyers have always had a buy cycle, starting at the point they perceive a need. Sellers have always had a sales cycle, starting at the point they spot a prospect. It used to be that these were in sync, either because the seller created the buyer's perception of need or because the only way for buyers to pursue their desire was to contact a salesperson (frequently for product information). Now, the buy cycle is often well under way before the seller is even aware there is a cycle.

One doesn't have to look far for evidence that this is so. As part of a recent speaking engagement, we asked for a show of hands: How many people had bought a car in the past two years? About a third of the delegates had. We asked them to leave their hands up if they went to the Web for information on cars before they communicated with a dealership. Virtually every hand stayed up.

More Work, Less to Show for It

Sales is a numbers game: Given a quantity of leads, salespeople will convert only so many into meetings. Some percentage of those meetings will progress to formal presentations. And some fraction of those presentations will yield sales. Our survey data show all those numbers looking worse in 2006 versus 2005, continuing a trend of several years' deterioration. The net effect is that it now takes many more leads—and much more work—to win the same amount of business.

Sales leaders reporting that . . .

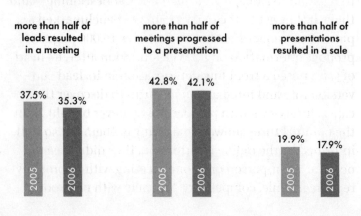

more than half of leads resulted in a meeting	more than half of meetings progressed to a presentation	more than half of presentations resulted in a sale
37.5% (2005) / 35.3% (2006)	42.8% (2005) / 42.1% (2006)	19.9% (2005) / 17.9% (2006)

The same finding shows up more scientifically in study after study, in both business-to-consumer and business-to-business commerce. Clearly, the tables have turned on negotiating power, and the advantage of information asymmetry is now the buyer's.

This is profoundly disruptive because sales reps used to live, more than almost anyone in a business, on the knowledge they held in their binders. They were the keepers of the data sheets, reference lists, white papers, and price lists. Whether the customer was a home owner trying to scope out the insurance he needed, a manager comparing commercial databases, or a space shuttle engineer specifying a transformer by weight and performance in certain temperatures—all used to require direct discussions with a vendor's sales rep, and sometimes over extended periods. Today, the information is available on the Web, not just from sellers but from other buyers and third parties. The three tasks we just named and countless others can be accomplished via the Internet in the time it took to write (if not read) this section of our article.

So sales forces find themselves in a challenging spot. Their reps arrive late to the party and must be prepared to respond to a deeply informed line of questioning—and that's if they get to the party at all. We benchmarked a plastics manufacturer that posted over 10,000 pages of product information on its Web site. Soon after, its head of sales noted a troubling deterioration in its lead conversion rate and hired an outside firm to discover the cause. Interviews with prospects who never bought from the manufacturer showed that many of them felt so well informed by the online information, they didn't see the need for an in-person or phone meeting with a company rep. Meanwhile, competitors, typically with no product

superiority and certainly no Web advantage, swept in
and walked off with the sales. Ease of access to the product information had actually turned into a barrier for the
company that provided it.

Elusive Decision Makers

Another deep trend behind the sales productivity down-
turn has to do with changes in how buyers make decisions. Salespeople have long been versed in the concept
of the "economic decision maker"—that single individual, particularly in a large deal, who holds ultimate
responsibility for the decision to buy. But such individuals are a vanishing breed. Replacing them are commit-
tees or multiple layers of approval all equally important
to the decision to move ahead. This is partly why the
length of the average sales cycle keeps increasing. In our
2004 and 2005 surveys, approximately 18% of the companies reported sales cycles of seven or more months. This
year, that figure approached 25%. On the opposite end of
the curve, only 42% of companies in the 2006 survey
stated that their sales cycle was three months or less,
compared with 51% in 2005. At the same time, the number of calls salespeople have to make before a decision is
made has risen over the past four years. Our interviews
underscored that these are not more calls on the same
people; they are more calls on more people, as deals
require more levels of sign-off and the support of more
stakeholders.

Priorities and Plans

Part of our survey's aim is to understand the challenges
sales leaders face, but the more valuable part is to discover how they are responding to these challenges, and

what actions yield positive results. As they plan initiatives for the next 12 months, sales executives are focusing their investments as shown in the exhibit "Top Sales-Management Priorities for 2006."

It comes as no surprise to us that lead generation is by far the top priority. Two benchmarking studies we conducted in the second half of 2005 underscored this finding. Both highlighted the importance of increasing campaign response rates, improving the hit rate in converting initial leads to qualified prospects, and making the most of leads when they are generated. All the needles are pointing in the same direction—toward reinventing how to get the attention of potential buyers.

For a salesperson, a steady stream of worthy leads is practically nirvana. Right now, our survey shows, about 20% of salespeople's time is spent on prospecting. The value of freeing up some of that time for pursuing already-defined opportunities is obvious. Also, when the flow of leads is more robust, the qualification of those leads tends to be more rigorous; the candidates that do make it into the sales pipeline tend to have shorter sales cycles, higher contributions to profits, fewer complications, and higher customer-satisfaction ratings.

This raises the question: What makes a qualified lead? For too many salespeople, the answer remains: anyone who can fog a mirror. Their bosses are hoping that better sales-talent management, more disciplined processes, and evolving technologies can put a finer point on things.

Depth of a Salesman

Sales executives understand that the new selling context has real implications for how they hire, train, manage, coach, and retain salespeople. Sales reps must now be able to dive deep, answering specific technical questions,

Top Sales-Management Priorities for 2006

We asked sales executives what areas they were targeting for improvement in 2006. More than anything else, better lead generation is their goal. This makes sense given that lead conversion rates have suffered. The more a salesperson can rely on a good lead-generation program, the less time she has to spend on low-return cold-calling.

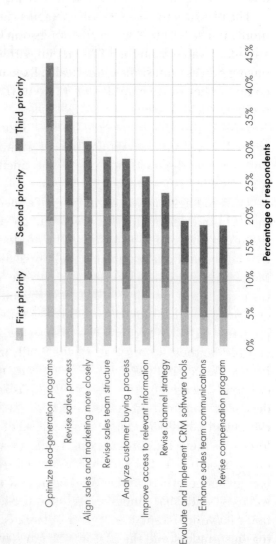

and fly high, providing purchase-justification arguments, solid business cases, and assessments of overall performance impact. They must provide more nuanced application knowledge and be able to "unhook" some of what buyers believe they know without alienating them.

The pressure to raise the salesperson's game is all the more intense because, when customers don't perceive any added value from their interaction with a seller, the buying process can shift dramatically. Executives at a computer hardware manufacturer told us that for one of their product lines, over 36% of 2005 sales came through "reverse auctions"—those race-to-the-bottom exercises where the customer says it will buy a certain number of units, and vendors with comparable products bid the price down to close the deal.

The good news is that companies' planned investments in training are up this year—and most of those resources will go beyond building the product expertise that has been the salesperson's traditional contribution. Many management thinkers before us have outlined the levels through which sellers must ascend in their customer relationships. We see this as a four-step progression: from vendor to preferred seller, then to consultant, then to contributor, and finally to partner. Each advancement pays off handsomely in increased credibility, access, margins, and repeat business—and decreased competition, price sensitivity, and sales-cycle length. But consider what's required of the sales force to achieve that progression. While a vendor needs only a good product or service, a preferred seller must have a higher level of understanding of how the seller will use it and what functionality is required. A consultant must understand a customer's business, a contributor must understand the customer's industry, and a partner must understand the customer's particular organizational issues. The shortage of salespeople knowledgeable and talented enough to attain those upper levels will become even more acute in the coming year, as our survey indicates an overall increase in net-new hiring. (See the exhibit "Sales Forces Will Grow.")

THE RIGHT ATTITUDE

As sales executives make these new hires, they tell us they are on the lookout for reps who are, or are willing to be, process oriented. We'll discuss what it means to be process oriented in the next section, but for now let us

Sales Forces Will Grow

Hold on to your best reps—more than two-thirds of our 2006 survey respondents said they were planning to increase the size of their sales forces.

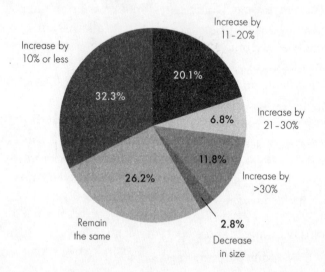

Increase by 11-20%: 20.1%
Increase by 10% or less: 32.3%
Increase by 21-30%: 6.8%
Increase by >30%: 11.8%
Remain the same: 26.2%
Decrease in size: 2.8%

share a basic piece of advice: Run, don't walk, from any candidates who say, "Look, if I don't make my numbers, you can fire me." They are expressly telling you they are not open to inspection or to the notion of continuous improvement.

But candidates aside, even some of your top producers currently on board may have this attitude, as well as another counterproductive impulse: "Nobody talks to my clients without me." For many years and in many ways, sales reps have fought to "own" their accounts and essentially broker customer relationships. All communication was through the sales rep, and exactly who was (or was not) involved in the dialogue on the buyer's side was often kept secret. Today, however, it's vital that a sales rep act as a facilitator between the two organizations, marrying up peer-to-peer discussions. So how do you change the hoarding behavior?

First, recognize that your reps are holding their accounts as bargaining chips. Then, reflect on why they feel the need to do so. If they were to foster communication between the company and their accounts, would the culture reward them? Or would it ask, "Since we're the ones doing the work of having all these conversations, why are we paying this guy so much?" Similar behaviors arise when companies roll out technology solutions like customer relationship management (CRM) systems and discover what a hurdle they face in user adoption. Sales reps think to themselves, "Hmm. If you know who I'm calling, have all their contact info, know the last time we talked and what we talked about . . ." Human nature tends to finish the thought with the worst fear: ". . . then you don't need me anymore." Again, because reps feel the need for bargaining chips, they withhold information and knowledge.

TIME IN POSITION

The expected increase in the number of new hires in 2006—and the experienced reps being targeted—should also serve as a warning. Smart sales executives are putting programs and policies in place to retain their best talent. Doing so has clear advantages. Our survey indicates that the greater the average tenure of the sales staff, the higher the percentage of reps making quota, the higher the average deal size, and the shorter the average sales cycle.

This year, we benchmarked several companies that were focusing on sales staff retention. For example, a publishing firm has a program that allows the top 10% of its reps (based on the previous year's performance) to hire their own administrative people for the coming year and bill the firm for the expense. This makes these stars even more productive and has brought their turnover rate down to 0%. A software firm is working to make sales a true life-cycle profession. Its new job structures allow salespeople to progress as individual contributors, as opposed to going into management to advance their careers. Other companies are motivating their sales support staff to stay in their jobs, too. One technology company, in the course of conducting customer satisfaction reviews, found that clients' ratings were often directly related to the tenure of technical support people working on their accounts. The company's compensation system, however, was encouraging those tech reps to move into other jobs, in development, technical marketing, or training. The firm changed that system by providing financial incentives for tech reps to continue working within established client relationships.

Process Prowess

Among sales management priorities, revising the sales process isn't far behind the top priority of generating more leads. But having a process is not the same as using a process. In our 2006 survey, 39% of respondents said that less than half of their sales force regularly uses the process the company has laid out as its standard, and another 31% said the standard process is followed by fewer than three-quarters of their reps. Having worked with many sales organizations, we've come to believe there are four levels of process prowess.

Level 1 companies may be perceived as being antiprocess, though what they really lack is a single standard process. Everyone does his own thing his own way. Being Level 1 does not mean a company is unsuccessful, but it does mean it is unpredictable.

Level 2 companies expect their salespeople to follow a process, but use isn't monitored or measured. This describes nearly half of the firms in our survey.

Level 3 companies typically enforce use of a standard process, sometimes religiously, but because their monitoring strictly looks backward, they are still susceptible to miscues and missteps in a constantly changing market.

Level 4 companies dynamically monitor and provide feedback on reps' use of the standard process. These organizations modify the process when they detect even minor changes in market conditions.

Level 4 companies are rare, but we found that they are formidable competitors—especially when they have also implemented CRM systems. As shown in the exhibit "Process Pays Off," their performance ratings tend to be much higher than those of the rest of the survey population.

Process Pays Off

We asked survey respondents about their sales organizations' performance along six important dimensions. Separately, we assessed each company's capabilities in sales process management. Note the huge performance differential between the organizations we found to be at Level 4 in their process prowess and the rest of the pack.

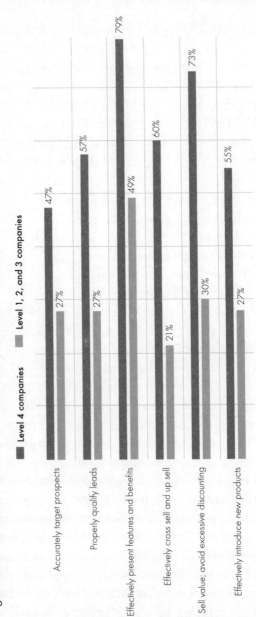

■ Level 4 companies **■ Level 1, 2, and 3 companies**

Accurately target prospects — 47% / 27%
Properly qualify leads — 57% / 27%
Effectively present features and benefits — 79% / 49%
Effectively cross sell and up sell — 60% / 21%
Sell value; avoid excessive discounting — 73% / 30%
Effectively introduce new products — 55% / 27%

Percentage of companies reporting "very good" or "world-class" ability

BUYERS HAVE A PROCESS, TOO

While a surprising number of companies do not formalize their sales processes, those that do typically define the seller's steps in the process. We suggest that companies go even further and keep track of the actions required of *buyers.* Such actions might include explaining why the opportunity is critical, outlining timing and budget, identifying key buying influences, offering to make introductions, and detailing purchasing and approval processes.

Why bother? As a seller, every step in the selling process is yours to make; it may seem like you control virtually all the actions. But there's one exception: You can't close the opportunity by yourself. Therefore, the truest test of your progress toward successfully closing a deal (and thus a more accurate basis for forecasting) is what the buyer is doing to advance the sale. The actions taken on the purchasing side to move a deal forward are worth defining and tracking.

MARKETING KICKS OFF THE SALES CYCLE

Third on the list of sales executives' priorities is to align sales and marketing more closely. Again, thanks to the wealth of online information available today, buyers are conducting early and detailed investigations before contacting any seller. So the first sales response is most likely not in sales' hands but in marketing's, where Web site responsibility most often falls. Other approaches like telemarketing and marketing portals create even more overlap as both functions inform prospects and qualify them. Where a clear boundary once existed between the two areas, things have now become blurred.

As a result, the sales force needs to be much more aware of marketing's activities and better communicate its own. Prospects and customers have a remarkably low tolerance for having to repeat themselves or to sit through repetitive presentations, especially when they have already taken the time to inform themselves of a seller's product and service capabilities.

For many sellers, the chief benefit of closer alignment between these two functions will be a better flow of information around leads. Salespeople constantly complain to marketing that there aren't enough leads. Marketing typically responds by asking, "What happened to the leads we gave you?" Every lead has a life, and there's no reason the status of each should not be known by both groups. And this, conveniently, brings us to the topic of technology.

Technology and Knowledge

Starting with the first contact management programs, evolving to sales force automation, and eventually morphing into customer relationship management, countless hours and dollars have gone into applying technology to sales. Early efforts focused primarily on efficiency improvements—doing things faster. Today's efforts focus more on effectiveness—doing things better. Our survey indicates new investment will be concentrated in CRM applications, sales knowledge management resources (including subscriptions to information-mining services, internal document-management portals, and internal tools for sharing best practices), and collaboration through technology (for instance, Web-based meetings, instant-messaging capabilities, and computer-delivered training). Just as important, we learned from current users of these applications that they are becoming easier to install and manage and that end-user adoption rates are rising.

By far the most common use of CRM today is contact management. Salespeople are most interested in having a contact database, a calendar function, e-mail, and integration with document templates. CRM's early breakthroughs—like the ability to generate a form letter drawing on designated fields and formatted with no extra spaces—now seem quaint. Today, CRM's automated processes usher contacts through predetermined paths using branching logic (for example, if no response to last mailing, send letter B; if contacted by phone, send letter D), literature fulfillment, and more.

Still, most of these functions are focused only on efficiency. Many of the very latest features, specifically analytics and dashboards (like graphical displays of data), are making processes more effective. They allow sales leadership to monitor things like aging reports for opportunities in the pipeline for longer than the mean cycle time; opportunities that have jumped several process steps, then stalled out; fallout patterns (steps at which opportunities have dropped from the pipeline); and prospect-quality ratings. How many metrics can be ginned up (think baseball fans' love of inconsequential stats) isn't as important as how many of them are leading indicators of future sales performance.

The established order remains: Get your process straight, then automate. Determine first what the high leverage points are (for example, sharing best practices, increasing order accuracy, and following up on marketing campaigns effectively) and then prioritize them. Most of what has been captured and stored in call reports, forecasts, win/loss reports, and CRM systems is data. And most of this is not useful because historically there was no well-defined process behind the data creation to ensure consistency. (See the exhibit "Where CRM Falls Short.") If you doubt this, consider how a typical sales manager responds to a set of reps' forecasts. His or her first reaction is to think, "I know that Ted's 60% is different from Suzie's 60%, which is different from Jim's 60%."

Having a process in place that defines what 60% means and that, with managerial oversight, is uniformly and correctly applied provides the basis for solid *data*. Having an application—be it business intelligence, data-mining tools, or analytic capabilities built into the CRM application—to grind through those data produces *information*. Categorizing and storing this information so that it is both accessible and actionable leads to *knowledge*. Creating a culture that rewards sharing and recognizes contribution brings all these components together to produce a competitive sales and marketing organization.

The Art of Selling

We often follow up with companies where we have conducted formal sales training. In one such company, we had equipped the salespeople with a form to use in their work. The form tied together several concepts taught in the course and, by doing so, could quickly reveal the strengths and weaknesses of a given sales opportunity. On our return, we discovered that their use of the form was not exactly rigorous. The vice president of sales hedged a bit, saying, "We're not religious about using the form. I mean, we tend to use it on bigger deals. . . . Some reps use it more than others. . . ."

Rather than simply rehash the concepts, we asked the sales reps to go through their files and desk drawers and

Where CRM Falls Short

A customer relationship management system is only as good as the data it draws on. So perhaps it's no surprise that the demands of populating a large-scale database and keeping it up-to-date constitute the biggest challenge in CRM projects. Progress on that front would no doubt address the second greatest hurdle: getting salespeople to use the system. Indeed, the two go hand in hand.

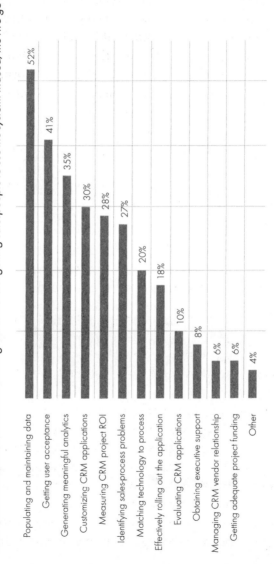

Populating and maintaining data	52%
Getting user acceptance	41%
Generating meaningful analytics	35%
Customizing CRM applications	30%
Measuring CRM project ROI	28%
Identifying sales-process problems	27%
Matching technology to process	20%
Effectively rolling out the application	18%
Evaluating CRM applications	10%
Obtaining executive support	8%
Managing CRM vendor relationship	6%
Getting adequate project funding	6%
Other	4%

Percentage of respondents

find any forms that had been completed during campaigns that year. Thirty reps managed to produce a few forms each. Our instructions were simple: "These forms are your equivalent of game films. Together, they cover nearly a hundred deals you pursued this year. Divide them up into wins and losses and look at them. Figure out what they're trying to tell you."

We share this story because the "films" taught us something. Unbelievably, between deals won and lost, there was no difference in what we thought was a key metric: the reps' success in getting to the top decision maker. However, in those deals that had been won, reps had early on and continuously made clear that they wanted and were trying to get to that decision maker, and they had articulated why that was important. It appeared that their clear and ongoing efforts to get to the decision maker produced positive pressure on the outcome of those deals even though, in many cases, the reps never actually got to that key individual.

For two sales experts who have spent years gathering data, it was one of those counterintuitive findings that keeps the job interesting. It was tempting to fall back on that classic conclusion—that selling is a science, except when it is an art. But we know that the best selling is now highly automated and process oriented, and that careful measurement produces insight and continuous improvement. And so another temptation prevailed: Here was a fresh hypothesis about selling. Given sufficient data, we could test it.

Originally published in July–August 2006
Reprint R0607C

Better Sales Networks

TUBA ÜSTÜNER AND DAVID GODES

Executive Summary

ANYONE IN SALES will tell you that social networks are
critical. The more contacts you have, the more leads
you'll generate, and, ultimately, the more sales you'll
make. But that's a vast oversimplification. Different configurations of networks produce different results, and the
salesperson who develops a nuanced understanding of
social networks will outshine competitors.

The salesperson's job changes over the course of the
selling process. Different abilities are required in each
stage of the sale: identifying prospects, gaining buy-in
from potential customers, creating solutions, and closing
the deal. Success in the first stage, for instance, depends
on the salesperson acquiring precise and timely information about opportunities from contacts in the marketplace. Closing the deal requires the salesperson to mobilize contacts from prior sales to act as references.

Managers often view sales networks only in terms of direct contacts. But someone who knows lots of people doesn't necessarily have an effective network because networks often pay off most handsomely through indirect contacts. Moreover, the density of the connections in a network is important. Do a salesperson's contacts know all the same people, or are their associates widely dispersed? Sparse networks are better, for example, at generating unique information.

Managers can use three levers—sales force structure, compensation, and skills development—to encourage salespeople to adopt a network-based view and make the best possible use of social webs. For example, the sales force can be restructured to decouple lead generation from other tasks because some people are very good at building diverse ties but not so good at maintaining other kinds of networks. Companies that take steps of this kind to help their sales teams build better networks will reap tremendous advantages.

ANYONE IN SALES will tell you that social networks are critical: The more contacts you have, the more leads you'll generate and, ultimately, the more sales you'll make. While there's some truth behind that thinking, it's a vast oversimplification. Different configurations of networks produce different results, and the salesperson who develops a nuanced understanding of social networks will outshine competitors.

The salesperson's job changes over the sometimes lengthy course of the selling process, with each phase requiring its own particular set of abilities. The skills involved in finding a lead don't apply to, say, closing a deal. Moreover, each stage requires the salesperson to build and use a different kind of social network. A grouping of prospects, for instance, has little in common with the network of experts who might be needed to convince a customer to finalize a purchase. Yet few managers, and even fewer salespeople, know how to manage their networks efficiently.

To better understand sales networks, it's helpful to view the sales process as four distinct stages: identifying prospects, gaining buy-in from potential customers, creating solutions, and closing the deal. Success in the first stage depends on the salesperson's acquiring precise and timely information about opportunities (ideally, ones that competitors don't know about) from contacts outside the seller's organization and in the marketplace at large. In the next stage, the salesperson needs to map the prospect organization and secure meetings with key decision makers so that the selling firm gets the serious consideration it deserves. That involves knowing who in the prospect company makes the decisions, who has influence, and what the potential customer's underlying problem is. Because answers must come from within the prospect, the salesperson needs people inside that organization to help him achieve his goals.

In the third stage, the salesperson comes up with a solution for the prospect, but rarely on his own. Success here depends on the seller's ability to identify where the components of the solution reside in his own organization—and on his skill at mobilizing and coordinating these resources. At the final stage, closing the deal, the salesperson's job is to remove as many of the customer's uncertainties as possible. The prospect wonders: Is this truly the best solution? Can this company deliver it? Will the company be around in two years? Will the salesperson answer the phone when things aren't working out? The prospect will want to speak with other customers who can shed light on the risks, so the salesperson needs to mobilize contacts in prior sales to complete the deal.

In each stage, the salesperson's efforts can be boiled down to two essential and complementary types of network-management actions: managing the information flow and coordinating the efforts of contacts. Some stages require more of one type than the other. In fact, the more information managing that's required, the less coordinating, and vice versa. (See the exhibit "Different Networks for Different Tasks.")

Thus it's obvious that salespeople's individual skills—cold-calling efficiency, consultative abilities, and product knowledge—are necessary but not sufficient. If salespeople are to succeed, they need the resources embedded within social networks; that is, access to the right information, the ability to disseminate it to the right people, and the power to coordinate the efforts of groups of people to deliver value to the customer. If you're a sales manager, you need to help your team build and maintain the right webs of contacts. In this article, we introduce a framework for systematically managing these all-important social networks.

A Closer Look at Social Networks

The term "social network" refers to a person's set of direct and indirect contacts. Consider Bob, an industrial chemicals salesman. At his previous company, he worked with Jim, Andy, and Brenda, procurement

Different Networks for Different Tasks

As a sale progresses through its four stages, the salesperson uses different kinds of social networks, and his or her job gradually shifts from gathering information to coordinating people's actions.

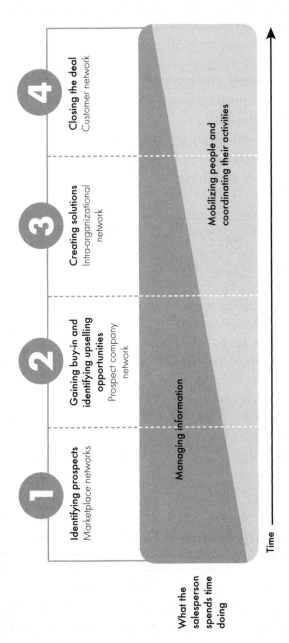

1 Identifying prospects
Marketplace networks

2 Gaining buy-in and identifying upselling opportunities
Prospect company network

3 Creating solutions
Intra-organizational network

4 Closing the deal
Customer network

What the salesperson spends time doing

Managing information

Mobilizing people and coordinating their activities

Time

managers at three different detergent manufacturers. He collaborated on numerous deals with each and shared an occasional beer after work to let off steam about workplace stress. Once, when Jim ran into problems with a supplier, Bob stepped in to fill the order. He also provided assistance to Andy and Brenda on numerous occasions. Bob can now call on these direct contacts if he needs help finding names of prospects for his efforts to upsell within their companies or if he needs a good word about his products to pass along to a new prospect.

Managers often view sales networks only in terms of numbers of direct contacts. But someone who knows a lot of people doesn't necessarily have an effective network, because networks often pay off most handsomely through indirect contacts. If Bob wants to garner a share of orders for a new line of detergents that Jim's company is developing, he'll need to persuade the chemists there to use his product in their test formulations and technical trials. So he can ask Jim if he knows anyone in R&D and get a personal referral to a chemist. The more people Jim knows in the firm, the more valuable he is to Bob.

The density of the connections in a network is another important characteristic. Do a salesperson's contacts know all the same people, or are their associates widely dispersed? Dense networks are suited to certain types of tasks, sparse networks to others. For example, Ron Burt, a professor at the University of Chicago's Graduate School of Business, has shown that sparser networks are better for getting access to unique information. If Bob's contacts Andy and Brenda aren't friends with each other, there's a good chance they have different information. The more dense a network (if Andy and Brenda are friends), the greater the likelihood that contacts will know the same people and hear the same news. Because relationships are not "free" to maintain—Bob has to call both Andy and Brenda from time to time and give them assistance when they ask—a salesperson with two redundant ties might consider cutting one of them.

Dense networks are more desirable for coordination purposes, as researchers such as Jim Baron at Stanford and Joel Podolny, now dean of Yale's School of Management, have shown. When Bob needs Andy's and Brenda's efforts to be coordinated and consistent, he's better off if they are friends than if they are not. If Bob counts on Andy and Brenda to tell new prospects about him, he wants them to say the same things. The closer their friendship, the more likely they are to share a similar perspective and speak with a common voice.

Most salespeople cultivate ties within four social networks: *Prospect networks* include the key decision makers in the prospect firm as well as people in its purchasing and engineering groups; these webs also include other influencers inside and outside the prospect firm. *Customer networks* consist of individuals from current clients. *Marketplace networks* comprise former colleagues, members of trade associations, and other actors in the marketplace (such as local real-estate agents) with whom salespeople maintain relationships. Contacts with representatives at other firms selling into the same customer base are particularly interesting components of this network, because those reps may have similar motivations but are not competitors. Finally, salespeople cultivate ties to individuals within their own organizations. These engineers, managers, marketers, manufacturing experts, and sales reps make up a salesperson's *intra-organizational networks*.

Matching the Network to the Task

If salespeople and managers understand how networks function, they can pinpoint the most effective network configuration for each stage of a sale and take the actions necessary to create it.

IDENTIFYING PROSPECTS

Many salespeople waste a great deal of time cold-calling or trying to breathe life into old leads. That's because they can't see clearly into prospective firms to know when the companies are getting ready to buy. The right network strategy can make the process of finding good leads much easier.

Let's look at prospect identification at Arrow Electronics, the *Fortune* 500 electronic-components company. Most of Arrow's orders are for ongoing applications at existing clients. Customers tend to remain loyal to suppliers once they have sourced components for particular products, so big sales opportunities arise only when a manufacturer develops a new product.

For Arrow's salespeople, then, the ability to identify firms that are starting product development cycles is a precious commodity. But prospects keep their product development activities secret to thwart competitors and to keep customers from canceling purchases of the existing version in anticipation of the next release. So how does Arrow discover which company is likely to be the next big buyer of components?

Some of Arrow's most effective salespeople rely on leads from nontraditional sources. Since one of the first things a start-up company does is lease office space, a real-estate agent may know about a new rollout before anyone else. Smart salespeople, therefore, cultivate ties with people in the realty network. Engineers formerly with existing Arrow customers are also good sources of information. Thus, Arrow's salespeople who keep up with their prior engineering contacts get leads before their competitors do. To put that into networking language, salespeople looking for new and unique information should cultivate broad marketplace networks. These direct contacts will be most beneficial in a sparsely structured network, where each can connect the salesperson to many different indirect contacts. The sparse web captures wider information than a densely woven network of contacts would. (See the exhibit "Identifying Prospects.")

The principle that information access is maximized in sparse marketplace networks holds true whether we're talking about selling electronic components or professional services. John Burgess, a partner at Boston's largest law firm, Wilmer Cutler Pickering Hale and Dorr (known as WilmerHale), relies heavily on his marketplace network to identify firms that will be interested in his expertise in cross-border IPOs. Investment bankers usually see IPO deals before attorneys, because bankers are the first people hired when a firm begins to think about going public. The more bankers Burgess knows, the more likely it is that one of them will lead to unique information.

GAINING BUY-IN AND UPSELLING

Once a salesperson has identified an opportunity, she needs to do two things: educate the prospect company about her firm's products or services and acquire more detailed information about the prospect and its underlying problem. Thus, she isn't just trying to maximize information inflow as she was during opportunity identification. She now needs to convince her initial contacts to invest time in educating her on their firm and introducing her to other people in their organization. (See the exhibit "Gaining Buy-In and Upselling.")

Asking an initial contact to introduce her to someone or to endorse her or her proposal is very different from simply asking for information. The contact isn't going to put himself on the line unless he's sure she won't jeopardize his reputation. So instead of building multiple nonredundant contacts—as she did in the marketplace

1 Identifying Prospects

A salesperson's network for finding new leads in the marketplace should be made up of contacts who know different people. That way, each direct contact can connect the salesperson to diverse indirect contacts, creating a wide web.

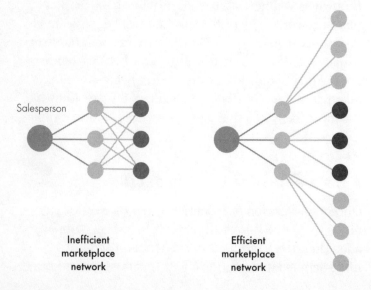

Salesperson

Inefficient
marketplace
network

Efficient
marketplace
network

network—the salesperson needs to establish fewer, stronger ties in her prospect network.

That is no easy task, as Hewlett-Packard's Computer Services Organization discovered in the mid-1990s. The unit had planned initially to penetrate new accounts by satisfying the (essentially commodity) hardware reordering needs of purchasing managers and then use those initial contacts to open the door to the IT department, where it could sell more complex hardware. HP planned to leverage *those* contacts to build relationships in the C suite in order to sell lucrative consulting projects. This foot-in-the-door plan failed because managers in customer companies derive a certain power from being

2 Gaining Buy-In and Upselling

In this stage of the selling process, the salesperson must build relationships with people in the prospect company beyond his or her initial contacts.

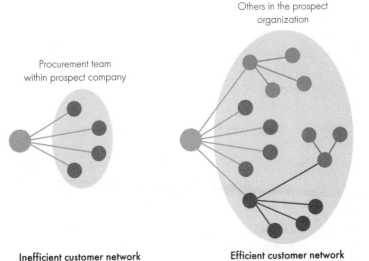

Inefficient customer network

Efficient customer network

connected to the supplier and all the benefits the supplier's salesperson brings. Contacts at customer firms didn't want to risk losing that power by allowing sales reps to call on other people in the organization. Had HP's sales managers spent more time evaluating the underlying prospect networks, they might have foreseen that their client contacts would not necessarily help them move higher in the organization.

In this stage, then, it's crucial for the salesperson to map out the prospect organization network and understand how it works. If he can determine who wields influence, he can devote his time and energy to cultivating ties with those individuals so that they can help him gain buy-in from the official decision makers.

Upselling is similar in some ways to gaining buy-in. To create more deals within existing clients, salespeople must focus on building new relationships within their prospect networks. They should study the client firm to identify brokers: people with multiple diverse contacts inside the organization. Brokers can provide the salesperson with a host of indirect contacts who, if tapped efficiently, can lead to a mother lode of information.

To find a broker, a salesperson must evaluate the nature, structure, and shape of the networks in the target firm. Who has formal authority? Who has informal authority? Who has access to information? Who always seems to know where to find things, people, and funding? Over time, the salesperson will be able to locate the most influential brokers. When he does, he should invest significantly in building relationships with them.

CREATING SOLUTIONS

A salesperson lands an account by developing a solution tailored to the customer's unique business problem. Her ability to bring precious, hard-to-find technical knowledge to the customer can make or break a deal. Because she cannot possibly know everything herself, she must rely heavily on the expertise located within her intra-organizational networks. (See the exhibit "Creating Solutions.")

In electronics sales, for example, a single motherboard might include hundreds of components, each of which is offered by many suppliers. Most of the components, moreover, become obsolete in less than a year. When a customer asks for help on the design of a new board that is to be installed in, say, airport autoflush toilets, what's the salesperson to do? She needs a sparse intra-organizational network that will link her to a diverse range of technical experts within her company. If she has built the right web, she can find the right expert quickly. She can create huge value by using intra-organizational networks to locate the right information and deliver it to the customer on demand.

When creating solutions, a salesperson is rarely able to simply tap his network for information. He must also act as a broker and assemble an ad-hoc team of experts, coordinating the efforts of people who may not have met one another before. The autoflush toilet, for instance, requires several types of engineering experts: specialists on a particular sensing device and generalists who know about compatibility issues with newly designed chips. The salesperson who can connect the far-flung nodes and create a smaller, dense network focused on the task at hand will be more effective.

CLOSING THE DEAL

By the time the salesperson has made it to the last stage of the sales process, he has demonstrated the product,

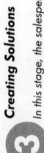

Creating Solutions

In this stage, the salesperson first develops a sparse intra-organizational network, which gives him or her access to diverse expertise. Next, the salesperson connects the experts in a dense network to maximize the coordination of their efforts.

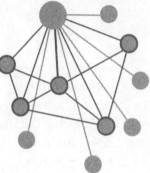

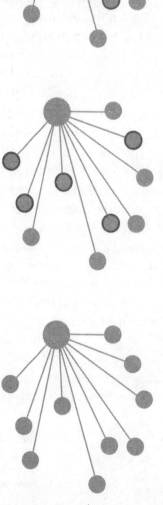

Build a sparse network

Pick the right experts

Connect them to make
an efficient network

held scores of face-to-face meetings, and exchanged hundreds of e-mails. The prospect has kicked the tires and taken a test-drive but is worried about what will happen after 50,000 miles of driving on his highway, the way he drives. How should the salesperson respond to that worry? He needs to find someone who drives just like the prospective client. In other words, he needs to provide references. (See the exhibit "Closing the Deal.")

At data storage giant EMC, for instance, a salesperson might be asked by a buyer from an airline: "How will EMC's storage system work with my applications? How will it interact with my IT infrastructure? How will EMC respond to my problems when I call?" The salesperson must then mobilize his network of past customers to find another airline with similar (or, better yet, the same) applications, infrastructure, and problems and must put people from the old client in touch with individuals at

---

4 Closing the Deal

In the final stage of the sale, the salesperson must mobilize a network of past customers and outside experts who can serve as references to help persuade the prospect to buy.

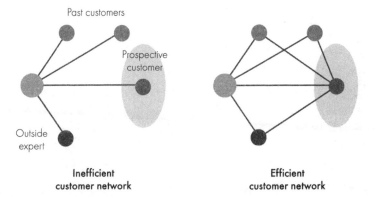

Inefficient
customer network

Efficient
customer network

the prospect. So in addition to being crucial for identifying upselling opportunities, a salesperson's customer network is very valuable for closing deals at other firms.

Experts outside the firm can be important in sealing a deal, too. An industry guru can have a powerful impact if, for instance, he can tout a product as the wave of the future.

Network-Smart Sales Strategies for Managers

We've shown that salespeople need to develop marketplace networks to identify new opportunities; that they need to build prospect networks to identify upselling opportunities and gain buy-in; that they must work their intra-organizational networks to create solutions; and that they need customer networks to close a deal. Moreover, the further along they are in the sales process, the denser their networks should be. In this section, we'll look at how companies and sales managers can use three levers—sales force structure, compensation, and skills development—to encourage salespeople to adopt a network-based view and make the best possible use of social networks.

SALES FORCE STRUCTURE

Clearly, the best way to ensure that your salespeople hear about new opportunities is to encourage them to build marketplace networks with many diverse contacts. Not everyone, however, is naturally good at that, so you should consider decoupling lead generation from other tasks. This is a common practice in certain industries. Many financial advisers, for instance, employ "bird dogs" who do nothing but identify leads. Some people are very good at building diverse ties but not so adept at maintaining other kinds of networks. They are extroverts who like to keep up with many people but lack the patience to connect individuals and coordinate their efforts. If they are allowed to focus on what they excel at, chances are they will get even better at generating diverse contacts and will thus produce leads much faster than people working at managing the ties within their networks. The people whose strengths lie in nurturing fewer but stronger relationships are likely to be far better at creating solutions and closing deals. If they can focus solely on those tasks, they'll probably become even more effective.

The downside to a decoupled structure is that it can work against the basic premise of networks. A network is effective because participants are willing to share with one another. They are part of what anthropologists call the "gift economy." A contact shares her resources with another on the understanding that she will gain access to that person's resources when needed. With a decoupled structure, it can be hard to keep the gift chain intact.

More specifically, lead generation is often tied to reciprocal favors delivered in later stages of the sales process. A manufacturer who gives a lead to a distributor's salesperson might expect that the manufacturer's line will be considered for incorporation in the solution when the salesperson gets to that stage. Decoupling lead generation from later stages can break this gift chain, because the lead generator has no opportunity to return favors. That situation could eventually lead to subpar performance by the marketplace network. One remedy is to create a database to track the source of each lead.

Then, in the closing stage, the salesperson would be able
to recognize what is owed to the referral source and
would be empowered to satisfy the obligation.

When it comes to gaining buy-in at prospects, managers can prevent salespeople from falling into the trap
HP found itself in. Managers might even make use of the
solution that HP ultimately came up with: restructuring
to access prospect firms through multiple sales forces. A
manager at a customer firm may not want to introduce
"her" salesperson to other people in the company, but
she'd be happy to introduce the salesperson's colleague
around. This approach can be very costly, however, so it's
appropriate mainly for high-value sales.

In the solution stage, a salesperson might justifiably
feel frazzled trying to cultivate the right networks for
creating various customers' solutions. There are several
ways managers can lighten the load. First, consider the
extent to which your firm's offerings have predictable
solution-creation needs. If solutions are relatively stan-
dardized, you should set up dedicated solutions teams
for major accounts, assigning support staff and salespeople on the basis of customers' requirements. Dedicated teams develop trust and commitment as members
become comfortable working together to complete complex tasks, often under great stress. This approach also
allows executives at the selling company to evaluate the
workings of the networks of experts within their organization—for example, the executives can monitor how
quickly people respond to a salesperson's call for help. Is
the sales force getting the support it needs? Which people work well together? Most important, establishing formal teams removes the burden of intra-organizational
networking from the salesperson. She doesn't need to

spend valuable time finding experts for every proposal. Management does all that networking for her.

If your offerings are complex and customized in an unpredictable way, consider an adhoc approach to team development, in which support people are tapped as needed. Managers can create an intranet listing of employees' areas of expertise and former work experiences so that salespeople assembling ad-hoc teams can easily find the most appropriate members. The salesperson can then send an e-mail to all the experts at once, describing the situation and requesting support. Instead of spending time finding internal experts, he can direct his efforts toward developing marketplace or customer networks. As an added benefit, managers will learn valuable information about support people's response rates to these requests and their speed in answering.

Another useful approach, common in professional services but applicable in other product domains, is to create groups that cut across functional areas. At the law firm Hale and Dorr (one of the predecessors to Wilmer-Hale), managing partner Bill Lee instituted "practice areas" that transcended traditional specialties such as corporate law, litigation, and tax law. The Life Sciences group, for instance, brought together attorneys from every specialty to discuss issues relevant to companies such as biotech firms. Members became part of an informal network, so that if a corporate lawyer from the group needed help on a litigation issue, he already had a relationship with a litigator through the group. Essentially, this approach established relatively sparse networks for members of each practice area.

Managers can also have an important impact in the last stage of the sales process. Prior clients can help close a deal, as we've pointed out, but salespeople often have trouble maintaining networks of potential references, who understandably don't want to be a part of helping rival firms make better purchase decisions. A sales manager can create an organizational structure that will motivate past clients to help. The way to do that is to assist the clients in building their own valuable personal networks. If a past client is a CIO, for example, the salesperson can help him meet other CIOs who might be useful not only in making future technology decisions but also in career moves—especially since the average CIO tenure is only 12 to 18 months.

Once a prior client has agreed to be a reference, you must decide who owns the right to contact him. Creating a team to manage and nurture the reference pool ensures efficient use of previous clients. If the CIO at, say, American Airlines will have the biggest impact on a prospect at either United or Delta, the salesperson will want to be sure that those are the places where the CIO's opinions are heard. A centralized structure minimizes the chances that any contact's privacy will be violated or his time wasted, and it thus helps prevent burnout, a common complaint among references. (Once customers agree to serve as references, salespeople may be less than diligent about protecting their privacy and respecting their time, especially when the reps are chasing deals at the end of the quarter.)

To reduce the risk that references will balk at helping a reference specialist with whom they have no prior relationship, managers can carefully transition each client to the centralized team. Such a handoff is fraught with risk, however. Success depends on the manager's making sure that the specialist positions himself as useful to the client and the client's own personal network and reputation.

COMPENSATION

A well-designed compensation plan will improve your salespeople's network management skills and maximize the flow of resources from networks. Since building the right kind of networks to foster leads is a time-consuming endeavor, consider offering explicit incentives for lead generation. Although this is an indirect approach to network building, it serves two important purposes: It increases the immediate benefits to salespeople from investment in their marketplace networks, and it makes a statement to the sales force about the importance the company places on leads and lead generation.

A system of financial incentives can also induce a salesperson to take the time to log each lead and all its associated information. Capturing detailed data—Where did the lead come from? What happened to it? Which contacts are providing the best information?—is extremely valuable for companies, especially in industries with high turnover. If the salesperson leaves, the lead doesn't disappear. Additionally, tracking data of this sort allows managers to ensure that salespeople are developing high-quality leads.

The salesperson's company can spur the creation of effective intra-organizational networks by compensating employees for supporting the sales force in creating solutions and closing deals. To discourage support people from aiding only the projects that seem easy to sell or only the salespeople who seem most likely to close deals, the company should base compensation on how many sales efforts are supported, the number of hours spent, and how quickly assistance is provided, rather than on how many solutions the support people help create. An added benefit of paying the back-shop employees a commission—even if it's not on the same scale as the salesperson's—is that you'll ease the resentment of the support people, who may feel they're doing all the work while the salesperson reaps all the benefits. Although that resentment stems from an underestimation of the effort that goes into selling, it can get in the way of a well-functioning intra-organizational network.

Some salespeople are inclined to hoard their most valuable reference sources to ensure that the contacts are available to them when needed. To counterbalance that inclination, some firms pay salespeople a small incentive, or "spiff," for every name added to a reference pool. An even more powerful tool for prying names from private lists is recognition: Give credit to the originator of a contact who eventually facilitates a closed deal.

SKILLS DEVELOPMENT

Senior managers must ensure that the network-based view of sales becomes the norm throughout the organization so that salespeople can readily learn network skills. Managers should thus promote an organizational culture that supports network-friendly activities. For instance, the company should sponsor social events to which salespeople can bring their contacts from various industries and contexts. Training is critical to transforming the firm into a network-aware organization. Frontline sales managers need to understand network concepts and be able to evaluate salespeople's efforts to implement network strategies. Moreover, the company's hiring and promotion decisions should be based on individuals' understanding of how to use networks effectively.

If your company has chosen not to decouple lead generation from the remainder of the sales process, there's an intriguing new technology that is worth investigating. Online networks—something like a Friendster for consultants and salespeople—may be extremely useful as a skills-development tool for people in your company who aren't naturally gifted at networking. These forums let users tap into a vast pool of contacts who are entirely different from their current contacts—that is, into a vast set of sparse network relationships.

Salespeople must be taught how to evaluate their own, as well as other people's, networks. Assessing networks is a crucial skill when it comes to securing buy-in at prospective clients. Salespeople should get used to asking themselves questions such as "Are my marketplace ties sufficiently diverse?" "Should I jettison a redundant contact so I'll have more time to build new relationships?" "Who in the prospect firm has the biggest and sparsest networks?" (Sometimes the contacts with the most valuable networks are hard to discern from the org chart.) "Who will be likely to promote the offering effectively?" "Who are the brokers?"

While we're not advocating an extensive (and costly) social-network analysis of every prospect firm, we would urge managers to give their salespeople the skills, tools, and foresight to evaluate factors such as the extent of a contact's connections in a prospect firm, whether the contacts are connected to one another, and how well the salesperson is positioned to make use of key influencers and decision makers.

Because the best way to get customers to serve as references is to help them build their own social networks, salespeople must be able to evaluate a contact's personality type as well as her networks. If she already has a broad and diverse network, she's likely to be highly motivated by the opportunity to expand her network, since she is clearly invested. If she frequently participates in conferences, she may well value the opportunity to heighten her public profile and make new connections.

Finally, an important element of maintaining a healthy customer network is recognizing that networks *need* maintaining. Most managers are comfortable training people how to do such important tasks as cold-calling and closing a deal, but few are confident in their ability to explain the best ways to simply keep in touch with contacts. E-mailing a contact every once in a while to "check in" or "just say hello" may not always be the best approach. Customers are likely to be irked by such a ploy. Managers should ensure that communications always add some sort of value. ENSR, an environmental consulting firm, produces a monthly newsletter that its salespeople send to their client contacts, many of whom are corporate managers of environmental affairs. It contains plenty of information about recent ENSR projects, to be sure, but it also provides data on industry trends that recipients may find useful.

ONCE YOU UNDERSTAND the four distinct stages of making a deal, it's clear that certain network configurations are better suited to certain tasks. In the earliest stage, a diverse marketplace network is best for identifying new leads. In the next stage, cultivating a prospect company network for access to the decision makers will help a salesperson gain buy-in. The third stage is all about coordination: Here the salesperson needs to forge ties among contacts in his intra-organizational network so they will work together to devise solutions for his prospect's unique problems. And to close the deal, the salesperson needs contacts from his customer network who can vouch for his good reputation.

We're not saying that cultivating all these networks is easy, but we believe that the salespeople who take the time to do it will reap tremendous advantages. Moreover, they don't have to go it alone. We've found that companies can make changes to their sales force structures, compensation plans, and training programs to institutionalize the network view of sales. Companies looking for better results should help their sales teams build better networks.

Originally published July–August 2006
Reprint R0607H

Leading Change from the Top Line

An Interview with Fred Hassan

THOMAS A. STEWART AND
DAVID CHAMPION

Executive Summary

MOST CEOS WHO SPECIALIZE in turning around struggling companies focus on costs. But for Fred Hassan,
chairman and CEO of Schering-Plough, the primary
focus in a turnaround is the top line. Since 2003, when
Hassan took the helm at the global pharmaceutical
company, he has overseen a remarkable recovery in
performance. And consistent with his philosophy, the
turnaround started with sales.

Considering sales reps as less than crucial to strategy, Hassan cautions, is a big mistake. At Schering-
Plough, he has concentrated on motivating and organizing salespeople to create trusting relationships with
doctors. "You have to differentiate the salesperson in the
customer's mind—just like you differentiate brands," he
explains. A doctor may see 60 pharmaceutical reps on
a regular basis but actually trust far fewer. To earn a spot

in this inner circle, Schering-Plough reps try to turn each customer encounter into an occasion to help doctors provide better care for their patients. Schering-Plough also restructured its sales forces so that reps carry not just one kind of product, as they do in most pharmaceutical companies, but several. Covering a broad range of treatments gives reps more ways to build value-adding relationships with doctors.

In this interview, Hassan discusses his success at Schering-Plough and his experiences at other pharmaceutical companies. During his career, he has built a reputation for being in tune with the front lines, as well as for reaching out to the managers who supervise salespeople. He has found that this level of personal attention not only makes reps feel respected but also gives him valuable strategic insights.

Most CEOs who specialize in turning around struggling companies focus on costs. Nissan's Carlos Ghosn, for example, was dubbed "le cost killer" by the French press. Tyco's Ed Breen and Aetna's Jack Rowe are both associated with headcount reductions. JPMorgan Chase's Jamie Dimon is celebrated for his "ruthless" approach to cost cutting.

But for Fred Hassan, chairman and CEO of the global pharmaceutical company Schering-Plough, the primary focus in a turnaround is the top line, and all his long-term corporate transformations have begun with the sales force. In part, that's a reflection of his professional roots. Hassan began his career in fertilizer sales, an improbable choice for the soft-spoken, almost self-effacing son of a Pakistani diplomat and a women's rights pioneer. The experience of those early days has influenced a long and successful career. Since 1997, when he took over the deeply troubled European-American drug giant *Pharmacia & Upjohn (P&U)*, Hassan has built a reputation for being in tune with the front lines.

It's clear that Hassan relishes a challenge. After completing P&U's merger with Monsanto in 2000, leading the new company—called Pharmacia—to health, and then steering it through its $60 billion acquisition by Pfizer in 2003, he was immediately tapped to take the helm at a struggling Schering-Plough. Over the past three years, he has overseen a remarkable recovery in performance, with improvements in every area of the business. Consistent with this CEO's approach, the turnaround started with sales.

For all these reasons, Hassan was a natural choice to be interviewed for Harvard Business Review's double issue on sales. HBR editor and managing director Tom Stewart and senior editor David Champion visited Hassan in early February at Schering-Plough's bright and airy headquarters in Kenilworth, New Jersey. During the conversation, it became clear that Hassan sees sales as the key to regaining control of the top line, which in his experience is more important than cost control as a long-term value driver. By focusing immediately on restoring sales force performance, a CEO can deliver a rapid turnaround in the numbers, which helps bankroll other essential changes while buying time for longer-term initiatives.

A critical challenge for a management team is to motivate and organize salespeople to develop the right kind of customer relationships. In the pharmaceutical industry, that means creating bonds of trust between sales reps *and medical professionals looking for better ways to care for patients. Indeed, the best way to gain market share in a crowded field is to be the salesperson to whom the customer turns for help. To make sure that he gets his vision across, Hassan works hard at reaching out to the frontline managers who supervise salespeople as well as interacting with the reps themselves. This unusually high degree of personal attention from a CEO not only makes the sales force feel respected but also gives Hassan valuable strategic insights. What follows is an edited version of the interview transcript.*

You're a CEO known for leading turnarounds from the top line. Why do you focus on sales?

The media like to point to a restructuring or a major strategic move as the key to a turnaround. But no restructuring or strategy will succeed long term unless you get control of your top line. Look at the U.S. auto industry. We can keep closing plants, but the real execution challenge is to reverse the market share slide. My first turnaround as CEO was with the failing Pharmacia & Upjohn merger. Although cost reduction numbers in the wake of that deal were largely on target, the bottom line was headed for a big shortfall because of a $2 billion gap in sales. The numbers were bad enough in themselves, but even worse, they had sent morale into a downward spiral, and the salespeople were among the most demoralized. They heard negative stories from customers on one side, and they got a bad vibe from the home office on the other. All this affected their numbers, which hurt morale even more. But because we focused on the salespeople early and got them to buy into the turnaround strategy, performance rebounded very quickly, which bought us time with investors.

In our industry, you really have little choice but to lead a turnaround from sales. You can always look good for a year or two by taking out some costs, but you have to be careful not to shortchange quality and patient safety. And you can't cut back on R&D because that's your future. You also can't lead a turnaround from the product side because R&D cycles in pharmaceuticals take ten to 15 years, so improvements you implement in drug discovery and development don't make much immediate difference. You have to deal with sales of the drugs you already have—or are about to have—and that window of opportunity is precisely defined because you know exactly how long you'll have patent protection. An effective sales force lets you make the most of that time. And, of course, it sets you up to take maximum advantage of any changes and improvements in discovery and development when those kick in later.

If sales is so important, why does it get such short shrift?

Most CEOs have financial, science, marketing, legal, or manufacturing backgrounds—and no sales experience. So they don't identify with the people who interact with customers. I think that's where the disconnect comes from. Paradoxically, marketing people are sometimes guilty of undervaluing salespeople as well. In the more extreme cases, they'll treat sales reps as just another conduit for the company's message, along with direct mail and advertising. But salespeople are much more than a passive medium. They are active representatives of the company and can influence people's perception of it through their ability to interact, to customize, and to build relationships with customers. Thinking of the sales force as anything less than that is a big mistake.

How do you avoid making that mistake?

You have to differentiate the salesperson in the customer's mind—just like you differentiate brands. The typical high-volume general practitioner is usually well known to all the drug companies. He probably sees as many as 50 to 60 different reps on a regular basis. He's got to decide who he is going to let into his inner circle of trust—and that may be only 15 reps. We work hard at being included in this circle. That means making each customer experience more than a typical detail call, in which the rep gives his scripted presentation and that's it. Standard detail calls program the doctor to treat the rep as nothing more than an information conduit. The key is to make the relationship value adding so that the doctor comes to trust our rep and looks forward to seeing him.

A trusted salesperson can be very helpful to doctors. Doctors are much more pressed for time than they used to be, which limits their ability to keep up with new developments. At the same time, patients now demand much more information, so doctors somehow have to stay abreast of medical advances and all sorts of other information. Fifteen years ago, patients wouldn't have been quizzing their doctors about the side effects of prescribed drugs. Today everyone wants to know about the drugs they may take, and the more sales reps can help doctors handle these questions, the more valuable they will be. That's why our reps differentiate themselves by focusing on science and on the concerns of patients—the doctor's customers. This means, of course, that reps must be forthcoming about the medicines they sell. And along with that knowledge, they must bring integrity and honesty about the science to their jobs if they're to build trust-based relationships with doctors.

How do you set salespeople up to seek out and develop those kinds of relationships?

We begin by attracting and retaining people who have the right attitude and behaviors. They must enjoy the professional aspects of selling or they won't become A players. We've also adjusted the salary and bonus ratio in the compensation package to give a relatively high salary component, which reduces the kind of hyperactive selling that undermines long-term trust building. And we inculcate our philosophy further through our sales training programs. We've also found that it helps to cover multiple therapeutic areas in servicing primary care physicians. At pharma companies, the primary care sales forces are often organized along therapeutic lines. A sales rep promotes only cardiovascular products or only central nervous system products, and so on. At Schering-Plough, in contrast, two years ago we reorganized most of our primary care sales force into six "mirrored" divisions, which are all the same in terms of structure. Each division has around 500 reps, and each rep serves one of about 500 territories, which means we have about 3,000 salespeople covering some 500 territories. Any rep in any division can, in principle, carry several kinds of Schering-Plough products, which gives us great flexibility in setting selling priorities for our reps and introducing new products. (See the exhibit "Organizing for Trust.")

If you had a therapeutically oriented sales force covering, say, allergy and oncology products and came up with

Organizing for Trust

Two years ago, Fred Hassan's management team instituted a major sales force restructuring at Schering-Plough. Today, unlike the sales forces at most pharmaceutical companies, Schering-Plough's salespeople are not organized by and large by therapeutic area. Instead, the company has structured its sales force according to doctors' needs, which means that individual sales reps carry products from multiple therapeutic areas. This structure not only increases the company's marketing flexibility but also gives salespeople more ways to make themselves valuable to their customers. The diagrams below are not an exact representation.

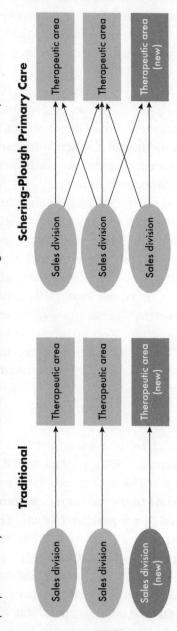

Traditional

A new sales division is required to support a new therapeutic area.

Schering-Plough Primary Care

The existing sales divisions can add a new therapeutic area to the products they already carry.

a new cardiovascular product, then you would either have to acquire a whole new sales team or force teams in other therapeutic areas to compromise their work to sell the new drug. We can just put a couple of our divisions on the job. During a large new-product launch, our mirrored divisions are especially powerful because we can have up to five sales reps meeting with a doctor. This kind of engagement would be much harder without our new structure. After the launch, our practices dictate that no more than two reps regularly discuss the product with any one physician.

I should add that once you've settled on a structure, you should keep to it for as long as possible. In theory, you could restructure sales territories every new selling period on the basis of new product priorities. A standard computer program can accomplish that. But it takes a rep 6 to 18 months to build a trusting relationship with a customer, so constantly breaking up relationships would turn every sales call into a detail call. That's why companies that rely on frequent restructuring to solve their sales problems usually end up in even worse trouble.

But how exactly does the new structure help build trust with customers?

It gives them more reasons to trust us. If you cover a broader range of treatments, you have a greater variety of ways to relate to the customer and more opportunities, therefore, to add value in the call. That gives you more opportunities to build trust. This is a subjective area, but we believe that our improving sales performance is linked to the increasing trust we are building in the doctor's office. A variety of measures, including physician feedback, suggests to us that our salespeople are steadily building trust with their customers. We also use data, such as in these slides, to sense how we're doing. (See the exhibit "Calling on Doctors.") If we get these types of things right, we believe our long-term value to shareholders will grow.

Has the emergence of other communication channels, such as the Internet and e-mail, affected the sales model in your business?

Not really. Personal interaction will be the core sales activity for a long, long time. That's how you build trust. That core activity will be more productive if you do good direct mail, have a good Web site, advertise well, or are visible at medical conferences and seminars. But anything extra you do thanks to new technology will tend to supplement rather than replace direct selling. Educating people through TV or print advertising, for example, gives them more questions to ask their doctors, which makes the doctors need trusted sales reps even more.

Let's look at the type of people who sell your products. Are they lone wolves or team players?

Obviously, they have to be good performers in their own right, but teamwork is essential as well. At the local district level, three or four different kinds of salespeople may need to share information and work together. If managed care colleagues have achieved approval for a product to be on a managed care formulary, other people on that sales team have to create the pull-through, and somebody else may have to get a hospital product onto a hospital formulary. The lone wolf approach works well in other industries, I guess—insurance or real estate, where you usually have to make only one sale to each customer. But it doesn't work in ours, where companies connect with customers in many different ways and repeatedly over a long period.

When you want to restore morale in a struggling sales force, where do you begin?

You begin with the district sales managers—the people I call "frontline managers." If I can get this management team to understand my vision and strategy, the rest of the sales force will follow. It is very powerful when you are able to gain buy-in from the frontline managers because they then become a dedicated extension of senior management's vision. Typically, a frontline manager will be responsible for 10 to 12 sales reps, who will be looking to her for confirmation that the strategy is really going to work. And it's not just her subordinates she'll influence. Salespeople in any industry are highly networked. People know what's going on in other companies. For all these reasons, we try to make the district managers our ambassadors from the center.

These managers were certainly an important factor in the first integration steps following P&U's merger with Monsanto in 2000. Very early in that process, I made sure that we got together with the Monsanto and P&U district managers in the United States and Europe. The point was to show them that instead of spending a lot of time on administrative issues, I was out there where it mattered. That helped motivate them and, in turn, the reps they managed, which meant that we didn't lose

Calling on Doctors

Pharmaceutical sales calls are monitored and analyzed by IMS Health, an independent consulting company. According to IMS's tracking system, visits by sales reps that are formally recorded by a physician's staff are counted as sales calls. On this measure, Schering-Plough ranks fourth, as the graph on the left shows. But IMS also tracks the outcome of the call by measuring the number of "contacts" with the physician and medical staff during the rep's visit. Examples of contacts include product discussions with doctors and various kinds of interactions with medical and office staff concerning products. On this measure, Schering-Plough tops the list, as the graph on the right shows.

Average customer visits (calls) per rep per day

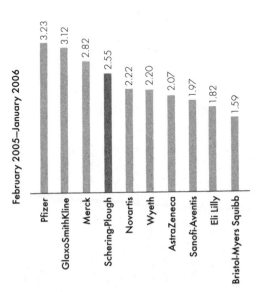

February 2005–January 2006

Pfizer	3.23
GlaxoSmithKline	3.12
Merck	2.82
Schering-Plough	2.55
Novartis	2.22
Wyeth	2.20
AstraZeneca	2.07
Sanofi-Aventis	1.97
Eli Lilly	1.82
Bristol-Myers Squibb	1.59

Source of call data: IMS Health, Integrated Promotional Services Audit.
Source of rep numbers: Verispan, Pharmaceutical Sales Force Structures & Strategies Audit.
Note: Calculations are based on an average of 17 field days per month.

Contacts per call

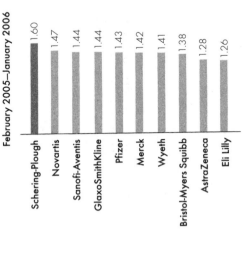

February 2005–January 2006

Schering-Plough	1.60
Novartis	1.47
Sanofi-Aventis	1.44
GlaxoSmithKline	1.44
Pfizer	1.43
Merck	1.42
Wyeth	1.41
Bristol-Myers Squibb	1.38
AstraZeneca	1.28
Eli Lilly	1.26

Source: IMS Health, Integrated Promotional Services Audit.

control of revenue during the merger process. In fact, we enjoyed healthy revenue growth.

How do you get salespeople to buy into your plans?

We make it a priority to educate people on the front lines about the company's strategy. That means letting them in on what I've been talking about with top management—I often end up in meetings with them using the same slides I showed to my senior management team or even to my board of directors. Linking them into strategy this way is really important because sales forces are often allowed to become detached from the center. In a way, I look on the salespeople as our first line of customers. If we can get them to feel that they're an important part of the company, then they won't immediately assume the worst if we have execution problems down the line with, say, the incentive plan. Then there are my CEO dialogues with the sales reps. These are regular meetings that I have with about ten sales reps at a time. The group is small enough that the reps can talk to me as individuals but big enough to generate a broad discussion. These meetings are always high-quality time. I've been doing this long enough now that many of the reps have had several meetings with me, which helps me see how morale has progressed.

I also regularly meet our customers in different settings, both with and without my sales colleagues. This serves two purposes. First, it teaches me a lot about the effectiveness of the sales process. Second, it gives me an opportunity to make our sales colleagues feel that the company understands their position and wants to help. I went on calls once in Manhattan and saw that the rep had to carry around a bag of samples on foot and on public transportation. What reps in a city need, clearly, is a bag with wheels. When I came back, I made sure that my trip report, which I shared with my executive team, included this observation.

Some might feel that the personal attention you give to the sales force is excessive. Do you agree?

Not really. The sales force has to be up there with R&D and the global functions—especially Compliance. And role modeling begins at the top. I routinely report on my experiences to my top cross-functional managers, and I encourage them to go on sales calls. Yesterday morning at a management committee meeting, I made a point of asking about a national district managers' meeting that I hadn't been able to attend. The fact that we spend time in the most senior committee of the corporation talking about a meeting with frontline managers makes a strong impression. I also personally see more senior managers in the sales divisions on a regular basis than those from other divisions, even though they are not direct reports. All this ensures that everyone in our organization appreciates the efforts of our colleagues on the front line, who have to make their six, eight, or ten calls a day and get past all the obstacles to connect with busy doctors.

As a CEO, do you get involved in making sales?

In some industrial marketing companies, landing the big contracts is a way for a CEO to make headlines. But I have no interest in usurping the role of my sales colleagues. I focus on being in tune with our people and assuring them that I'm behind them, that I care about them, that I care about the reputation and integrity of our company, and that what they do is important to the company and to patients. I think that is where I make a difference.

It's easy to see that American salespeople would respond well to your approach. Does it pose any special challenges outside of the United States?

Not in my experience. Once people are in small groups, the cultural stereotypes don't apply anymore. People in sales are naturally extroverted, and that proves to be stronger than any cultural stereotype. When I went to Japan for my CEO dialogues with our sales reps there, a lot of people thought that none of the reps would say a word to me. But within about ten minutes, they became very lively. Another time, when I was with P&U, I met some sales reps in a remote part of China. To my surprise, they told me that one of the benefits they most appreciated was the company's stock option plan, which we had just put the sales reps on. Most people at the time thought that only Americans would really value a stock option plan. And yet here were sales reps in the depths of rural China telling me they liked it.

If some marketing people have blind spots when it comes to sales, how do you change that?

Many marketing people in the pharmaceutical industry started in sales. But schisms can arise, especially in times of stress. Left unmanaged, people in the field might point a finger at people in marketing, and vice versa. You have to fight this. One of Schering-Plough's six formally identified Leader Behaviors is "shared accountability and transparency." We make concerted efforts to model and teach the right behaviors to emphasize just how important they are. In one of my former companies, we went to a sales and marketing meeting and handed out T-shirts with the words "sales" and "marketing" on the front without a space between them. This symbolized what we wanted the department to be.

We also have various business processes that ensure that both sales and marketing resolve any tensions early on in a new project. One of the most important is the Plan of Action (POA) meeting. These meetings can take place three times a year, and they require marketing people to work with district managers and sales reps to develop special sales programs. The marketing people elicit input and feedback from the salespeople to design the best possible program, and there's a lot of emphasis on teamwork. In the end, our ability to plan and then execute as a team has greatly increased as a result of this process.

Can you give us an example?

Sure. Let's say we were developing brochures to disseminate new approved clinical data on one of our products. From the very beginning, our market research colleagues would be speaking with customers to develop the initial messaging. We would then use a forum like the POA to involve the sales force in the early stages of the project— well before the brochures were finalized. This not only ensures that everyone buys into the brochure but also encourages the salespeople to actually use it with their customers. Once again, we've been able to give sales reps something they can talk about, and in so doing they will make sure that we get the information to the people who need to see it. A process like this takes more time on the front end, but I can tell you it's worth it.

Do you find that interaction with the front line generates any strategic insights?

Absolutely. The sales reps are usually the first to spot gaps in the product line. There was a case of this recently in our respiratory business. The sales reps had told me that they would like to be able to offer an antibiotic in addition to our antihistamine line. I remembered this request when the opportunity came up to access an antibiotic called Avelox, which is used to treat pneumonia. Licensing Avelox wasn't a very big deal in terms of its bottom-line effect, but its strategic fit was good. It allowed our salespeople to present a much broader range of respiratory products. It made the reps feel more relevant to their customers. I think they had started to feel that we weren't committed to respiratory products, so this move lifted their spirits and made them realize that we were serious about the area. If it hadn't been for their input, we would probably have passed on the Avelox opportunity, and Schering-Plough would have struggled longer in respiratory products.

What you hear from the front line can also be a great corrective to the prevailing wisdom. I worked at a company where the R&D people had developed a glaucoma drug for the Japanese market. The conventional wisdom was that because eye care was not a core business, the company should partner with a specialist Japanese distributor. We were all set to do this. But when I talked to our salespeople in Japan, they told me that being able to offer the glaucoma drug would really help them with their customers. They also believed they could do a better job than the Japanese distributor because they were better trained as sales professionals. We took the courageous step to give the product to our own people, which turned out to be a wise decision. The glaucoma product sold very well in its own right, and sales of other products also benefited because salespeople were motivated to do the best they could.

Originally published in July–August 2006
Reprint R0607G

The Sales Learning Curve

MARK LESLIE AND CHARLES A. HOLLOWAY

Executive Summary

WHEN A COMPANY LAUNCHES a new product into a new market, the temptation is to immediately ramp up sales force capacity to gain customers as quickly as possible. But hiring a full sales force too early just causes the firm to burn through cash and fail to meet revenue expectations. Before it can sell an innovative product efficiently, the entire organization needs to learn how customers will acquire and use it, a process the authors call the sales learning curve.

The concept of a learning curve is well understood in manufacturing. Employees transfer knowledge and experience back and forth between the production line and purchasing, manufacturing, engineering, planning, and operations. The sales learning curve unfolds similarly through the give-and-take between the company—marketing, sales, product support, and product development—

and its customers. As customers adopt the product, the firm modifies both the offering and the processes associated with making and selling it.

Progress along the manufacturing curve is measured by tracking cost per unit: The more a firm learns about the manufacturing process, the more efficient it becomes, and the lower the unit cost goes. Progress along the sales learning curve is measured in an analogous way: The more a company learns about the sales process, the more efficient it becomes at selling, and the higher the sales yield.

As the sales yield increases, the sales learning process unfolds in three distinct phases—initiation, transition, and execution. Each phase requires a different size—and kind—of sales force and represents a different stage in a company's production, marketing, and sales strategies. Adjusting those strategies as the firm progresses along the sales learning curve allows managers to plan resource allocation more accurately, set appropriate expectations, avoid disastrous cash shortfalls, and reduce both the time and money required to turn a profit.

W HEN A COMPANY LAUNCHES a new product, the temptation is to immediately ramp up sales force capacity to acquire customers as quickly as possible. Yet in our 25 years of experience with start-ups and new-product introductions, we've found that hiring a full sales force too fast just leads the company to burn through cash and fail to meet revenue expectations. Before it can sell the product efficiently, the entire organization needs to learn how customers will acquire and use it, a process we call the sales learning curve.

The concept of a learning curve is well understood in manufacturing. Employees transfer knowledge and experience back and forth between a production line and the purchasing, manufacturing, engineering, planning, and operations departments. Over time, the entire process becomes more effective: The more times a process is repeated, the more efficient it becomes and the lower its cost.

Start-ups and existing companies launching new products follow a sales learning curve that's analogous to the manufacturing learning curve but one that unfolds through the give-and-take between the company and its customers. As customers adopt and use the product, the organization modifies both the offering and the processes associated with making and selling it. (See the exhibit "Learning Processes for Manufacturing and Sales.") A large sales staff hinders more than it helps a company climb the curve. Instead of following conventional sales wisdom, the firm should focus first on organizing itself so it can learn from customers and respond to them.

It's important not to confuse the organization's sales learning curve with a salesperson's individual learning curve. Most companies expect sales reps to go from new employees to fully productive salespeople during their first months on the job, as they learn more about the product, the customers, the market, and the competition. The sales learning curve we are describing is separate from, and independent of, the individual learning curve and more comprehensive, involving all customer-facing parts of the organization: marketing, sales, product support, and product development. The improvements in sales yield that result from this organizational learning process affect all of the sales representatives, both new and experienced.

Learning Processes for Manufacturing and Sales

An innovative product does not arise fully formed from a flawless development process. It emerges from the give-and-take between all the departments involved in its creation—purchasing, manufacturing, engineering, operations, planning, and the factory floor. The same is true for the sales strategy that will bring that product to market. It, too, is an iterative process, one that involves all the departments that face customers.

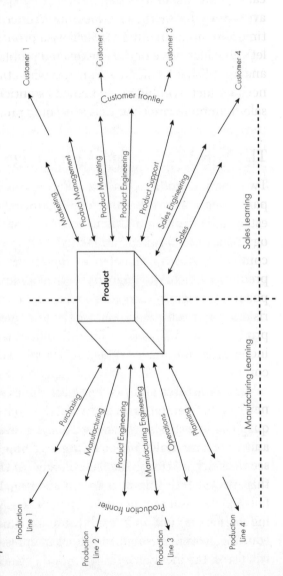

In this article, we will look at the sales learning curve as a framework for helping managers and investors develop thoughtful launch strategies, plan resource allocation more accurately, set appropriate expectations, avoid disastrous cash shortfalls, and reduce both the time and money required to achieve a profit. But first, let's consider some of the unexpected problems start-ups and established companies run into when they launch a new product—problems that could be anticipated if the sales function were viewed as a learning process.

The New-Product Sales Challenge

Twenty-five years ago, the major risk in creating a company (or in launching a brand new product from an established company) was the feasibility of the technology. Managers believed: "If we can build it, they will come." Today, the product development cycle is more predictable, thanks to the greater availability of subcomponents and robust development tools. So the biggest risk for most companies has shifted from getting the product to work to getting it to market. Entrepreneurs increasingly must ask: "When we build it, will they come?"

But if start-ups apply conventional sales wisdom to new-product launches and add sales capacity too quickly, the result is often disappointing revenue growth and a cash shortfall. (For an example of how that works, see the sidebar "How Big a Sales Force?" at the end of this article.) That's because the conventional wisdom fails to address a number of challenges involved in creating markets for unfamiliar products: the time required to educate customers about the offering and learn how they will use it, the inevitable design modifications needed to deliver a robust product that will fully satisfy customers, the identification and resolution of service issues, the development of a repeatable sales model, the selection of appropriate market positioning, and the design of effective sales incentives. Here's a case in point.

MIDCOURSE CORRECTION AT A START-UP

Scalix, a software company that develops e-mail and calendaring programs hosted on Linux, is one start-up that struggled to get its sales model right. The company's founders recognized that the underlying infrastructure of market-leading e-mail systems such as Microsoft Exchange was originally designed for work groups and had never been upgraded to efficiently support large organizations. They believed that the disruptive nature of the Linux operating system created a rare opportunity for a new supplier to enter the mature e-mail market with a solution that was more secure, reliable, scalable, and cost effective. Specifically, they aimed to cut total cost of ownership by 50% to 60%.

Scalix launched its product, based on Hewlett-Packard's OpenMail system, in July 2003. In early interviews, CIOs responded enthusiastically to the promised cost savings, so the company decided to expand its sales capacity quickly. Its initial strategy was simple: Recruit a high-powered sales leader with enterprise experience and sell directly to CIOs at large companies.

However, as Scalix moved deeper into the sales cycle at large corporations, the company encountered a number of unexpected problems. First, it became evident that the CIO was not the primary decision maker for purchasing e-mail systems. In many cases, the operations team one level down—the people who would be responsible for keeping the system up and running on a daily basis—rejected Scalix's solution. These department managers didn't want the headache of moving their Windows-based Exchange administrators over to Linux. And the Exchange administrators themselves viewed moving to Scalix as a career detour.

The second problem was closely related to the first. Scalix discovered that many large companies needed to get more comfortable with Linux before they would run e-mail on it. While a small group of people trained on Linux existed in most organizations in Scalix's sales pipeline, they were not working on e-mail. Early adopters, such as Amazon and eBay, were running only customer-facing applications on Linux.

The third problem was of an entirely different order and perhaps the thorniest. Scalix learned its product was not quite ready for prime time. CEO Glenn Winokur explained: "You come out, and you think you have a market-ready product. Then you discover that you really don't. You're 90% of the way there, but there's another 10% you have to iterate on with customers. From the time we came out and through all of 2003, we iteratively worked on pilots and trials with customers and learned the full extent of customers' requirements for enterprise-class e-mail."

Scalix faced such an uphill battle selling directly to large enterprises that after a few sales to small public sector accounts, the company corrected its course. In mid-2004, it overhauled its go-to-market strategy to hit the Linux evangelist and early adopter community first, with a particular emphasis on smaller targets in the higher education and public sectors, where Linux acceptance was strongest. To execute this new strategy, Scalix hired two in-house telesales representatives to drum up leads. With lower-priced salespeople and a compressed sales cycle, the new model offered much better economics than the original field sales approach. The revised sales strategy is working well. Scalix was named one of *Red Herring*'s 100 top private companies of North America in 2004 and 2005.

Such adjustments aren't unusual when companies interact with real customers deploying a product to do real work and in the process learn how to better meet their customers' needs. But Scalix could have saved scarce resources and learned important lessons far more quickly had it delayed hiring a traditional sales force and focused all customer-facing departments on learning from the beginning.

BREAKING NEW GROUND AT AN ESTABLISHED COMPANY

Established companies often make many of the same mistakes in launching a new product that start-ups do. They hire experienced sales talent far enough in advance of the launch to allow them to come up to speed (based on conventional sales wisdom), and then they sit back and wait for the sales team members to deliver their expected quotas.

In late 2001, Veritas Software, now part of Symantec, was a large software company that sold three major software products through an international sales force of more than 2,000 field employees. It was very good at selling successive releases of its existing products, but the company's track record in new categories was spottier. Although its signature file and disk management software was competitive in its features, many customers preferred a bundled hardware and software solution like those from EMC and Network Appliance. So Veritas decided to launch a new class of products, a set of software applications preconfigured to run on servers from vendors like Dell, Compaq, HP, and IBM. This bundled solution would offer the cost advantages of buying commodity PC server hardware from existing vendors together with a complete plug-and-play software package from Veritas.

The company's initial go-to-market strategy was to create an overlap sales force that would work closely with the regular software sales force. Both sales teams received commissions on the new product. However, a number of problems arose shortly after the launch. Veritas had expected the product to be completely developed and ready to go, but it was not yet either fully reliable or fully functional. This frustrated the regular sales team, which was used to selling mature products. Reps were compensated for sales of the new product but not enough to make up for the extra time and effort required. In addition, the new bundled offering was seen as a potential threat to the company's traditional hardware partners like Sun Microsystems, making them less likely to cooperate with Veritas at the field sales level. Understandably, savvy regular salespeople never enthusiastically supported the new product. Veritas abandoned the initiative a little over a year after its introduction because the revenue remained substantially below expectations.

Had Veritas better understood what was involved in the sales learning curve for this new venture, it could have anticipated and made provisions for these problems.

What the Organization Needs to Learn

Every business goes through a unique learning process, and each industry, company, and product has a different set of drivers. As the Scalix and Veritas examples show, the product will probably not have exactly the right features or work exactly the way it should at the outset. The sales and marketing processes may not be focused initially on the right customers. To traverse the learning curve, product development, marketing, and sales must resolve a host of complicated questions. The product developers, for instance, need to correctly determine which features would make the product valuable to customers. They need to make it easy to use, reliable, and efficient to service. Marketers need to correctly analyze the product's position relative to its competition. They need to segment its market. They need to develop packaging. The sales team needs to determine the number and type of distribution channels, develop a sales model, work up a sales pitch. The broad range of issues that all three departments must resolve to launch a successful product is summarized in the exhibit "What Goes into a Comprehensive New-Product Strategy." When you look at the length of the list, it becomes easy to see that launching a new product involves far more than ramping up a large sales force.

Gaining that knowledge, of course, doesn't happen all at once. Nor does it happen in a vacuum. It develops gradually: The company makes initial assumptions, which are modified iteratively as feedback comes in from early customers. The modified offering reaches even more customers, whose further feedback hones the product, the message, and the sales efforts—accelerating the company's progress along the learning curve. This process cannot be short-circuited by sending out an army of salespeople in an effort to gather more feedback more quickly: Many problems are discovered sequentially, revealing themselves only after some preceding issue has

What Goes into a Comprehensive New-Product Strategy

Launching a completely new product into a new market is not just a matter of hiring an army of salespeople and letting them loose once the product is created. Product developers, marketers, and sales staff need to resolve a host of issues:

Product development	Marketing	Sales
Completeness	**Positioning**	**Distribution channels**
> Features and functions	> Competitive analysis	> Number and type
> Interface to existing ecosystem	> Market segmentation	> Channel support and training
> Ease of installation	> Marketing messages	
	> Proof of value proposition (ROI)	**Sales force**
Correctness	> Packaging	> Sales model
> Value to customers		> Sales pitch
> Reliability	**Promotion**	> Training and development
> Ease of servicing	> Collateral materials	> Lead generation
	> Advertising, shows, and PR	> Technical support
Fit	> Customer testimonials	
> Ease of use		**Sales stage**
> Suitability for environment	**Pricing**	> Learning
	> Across market segments	> Development
	> Across channels	> Expansion

been discovered and addressed. Eventually, the company learns enough to reach a level of steady sales.

The Sales Learning Curve

Companies have long measured their progress along the manufacturing learning curve by tracking costs per unit—the more they learn about the manufacturing process, the more efficient it becomes, and the lower the unit cost goes. Progress along the sales learning curve is measured in an analogous way: The more a company learns about its product, market, and sales process, the more efficient it becomes at selling, and the higher the sales yield. "Sales yield" is defined as the average annual sales revenue per full-time, fully trained and effective sales representative. Typically, sales yield for a new product starts out slowly, accelerates for a while, and then flattens out as the product matures, in a classic S-shape curve.

The steepness of the curve—a measure of how rapidly product revenues reach the break-even point and then achieve targeted levels—varies substantially from product to product. For example, when the Palm Pilot was introduced, it created a whole new product category. The sales learning process was long and complicated, resulting in a sales yield curve that looked like the first curve in the exhibit "How Steep a Curve?" By contrast, the competing Handspring, a follow-on product in a now-established market, was launched with a "better, faster, cheaper" strategy, and its learning process was far quicker. Accordingly, its sales curve is shifted to the left and far steeper, resembling the second curve in the exhibit. For many new-product launches, the sales yield never reaches expected levels, or even the break-even

How Steep a Curve?

Progress along the sales learning curve is measured by tracking sales yield over time. As you might expect, the curve for launching a totally new product into a new market is much longer and flatter initially than one for introducing a variation of an existing product into an established market. Clearly, the longer the learning curve, the greater the revenue gap—that is, the longer it takes for sales yield to reach targeted quota levels. Setting expectations appropriately, therefore, can make the difference between pioneering a new market and aborting too soon.

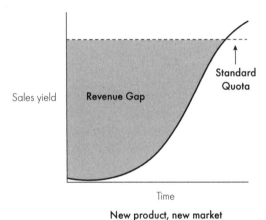

New product, new market

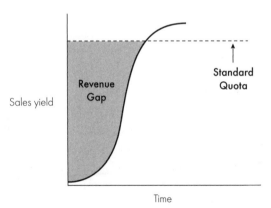

Follow-on product, existing market

point, resulting in cash shortfalls and premature death
for promising products.

   Tracking sales yield can be more challenging than
measuring manufacturing production volumes and costs
because revenue-generating activities tend to be less predictable than production. Still, applying the concept of a
sales learning curve allows you to understand where in
the learning process your launch is, so that you can
deploy your sales force, marketing efforts, engineering
support, and management time appropriately.

Sales Force Planning for Launch

The way to shift the sales learning curve to the left, and
reach the break-even point and profitability more
quickly, is to track sales yield over time and adjust your
go-to-market strategy as you move along the curve.
That's because the sales learning process unfolds in three
distinct phases—the initiation phase, the transition
phase, and the execution phase—as the exhibit "Ramping Up the Learning Curve" shows. Each phase requires a
different size—and kind—of sales force, and represents a
different stage in your production, marketing, and sales
strategies. The gateways from one stage to the next correspond to two markers of profitability level—the break-
even point and some targeted level of steady sales, which
we call the "traction point."

THE INITIATION PHASE

This phase begins when the product is ready to hit the
market, that is, when it has been beta tested, and lasts
until the break-even point—that is, when sales yield
reaches a point where revenue per sales rep equals the

fully loaded cost per sales rep. Typically, during this time, few customers will be willing to consider buying the product, and those that do will require significant incentives.

It's both unrealistic and potentially dysfunctional to assign large sales quotas in the initiation phase. The members of the sales team should be encouraged to focus instead on learning as much as they can about how customers will use the product so they can support engineering, product marketing, and marketing communications in perfecting both the offering itself and the go-to-market

---

Ramping Up the Learning Curve

The go-to-market strategy for a new product should unfold in three parts. The staffing and financial resources needed in the first stage, before the product is profitable, are very different from those needed in the second stage, when the product is being refined, and different again from those needed after most issues have been resolved and sales have reached a sustainable, predictable level.

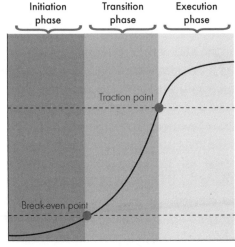

strategy and programs. A heavily commission-based pay plan is not only unlikely to achieve sales objectives but can inhibit learning.

It's also inefficient to hire too many sales reps in this phase. A small sales force not only keeps costs down but is more effective in supporting other parts of the company. Typically, three to four salespeople are enough to start the learning process and to make sure that the problems encountered aren't just the result of a bad hire.

The types of skills needed during this phase differ from those needed to sell more mature products. They include a facility for communicating with many parts of the organization, a tolerance of ambiguity, a deep interest in the product technology, and a talent for bringing customers together with various functional teams within the company. Salespeople must be resourceful, able to develop their own sales models and collateral materials as needed. We think of this kind of person as the "renaissance rep."

THE TRANSITION PHASE

Toward the end of the initiation phase, companies generally have acquired a critical mass of customers, and sales are beginning to accelerate. Once the sales yield equals the fully loaded expense per sales rep, it's safe to assume you've moved into the transition phase. This second phase lasts until the sales yield reaches a point where company management can see that the product has achieved real traction in the market.

What constitutes "traction" varies from company to company and product to product. Still, we've found that a useful rule of thumb is to consider a sales yield of twice the fully loaded cost per sales rep as the end of the transition phase. By this point, the company should have a pretty good idea of what to expect in terms of steady state sales yield for the product.

In the transition phase, sales management should focus on developing a repeatable sales model, refining market positioning, and adding sales capacity at a rate commensurate with the rise in the slope of the curve. The original renaissance reps should continue to stay focused on learning. The people hired at this stage—we call them "enlightened reps"—should be comfortable contributing to a still-evolving sales model but do not need to have the analytical and communication skills of the renaissance reps.

THE EXECUTION PHASE

Once sales management is confident that the product has achieved traction and is entering the execution phase, sales reps can be hired as rapidly as the company's management and financial constraints will allow. In this phase, when the formula for success has been developed and all of the support requirements for sales reps are in place, the company needs more traditional salespeople— what's known in the industry as "coin-operated reps"— who require nothing more than a territory, a sales plan, a price book, and marketing materials to bring in orders.

The Role of Marketing

Product marketing and marketing communications should ideally be the center of learning activities during the initiation phase. Marketing leadership is responsible for bridging the gap between customers, sales reps, and the engineering organization. Everyone on the marketing

team has to be knowledgeable about the product technology, able to understand customers and their needs,
and proficient at communicating with renaissance reps.
But success in this role requires more than just an understanding of the languages of these disparate groups and
individuals in the company. It requires substantial credibility to convince customers, sales, and engineering that
their needs will be accurately communicated to the other
parties. Marketing must hold the product itself to high
standards of completeness, correctness, and fit.

Once beta testing is complete, the company must
decide when to launch a marketing campaign. There can
be pressure to start the campaign early to support the
sales effort, but that's an expensive use of scarce cash
resources. What's more, it can distract the organization
from its primary learning goal and set false expectations
among the sales and engineering groups. Worse, a premature marketing campaign can set false expectations in
the marketplace that will be difficult to correct.

As the company tweaks the product and learns more
about the ways customers use it in the first two stages,
the positioning will evolve. Marketing communications
must develop a nimble launch schedule that can adjust
to the requirements of each stage by preparing collateral
materials that can be easily modified and by working
with media and other resources so they can respond
quickly once the final product and sales strategies have
been completed.

The Role of Engineering

Keeping the product development engineering team
intact at least through the initiation phase is essential to
the success of a new-product launch. This is a significant

challenge for both company executives and engineering management: After beta testing is done (and sometimes even before), the engineering organization typically turns to the next product. Cleaning up and making sure that existing products are complete and correct is not the most glamorous phase of product development. What's more, the reward systems in most R&D organizations encourage engineers to go on to the next challenge. But when companies allow those most intimately knowledgeable about a new product to move on, they slow down learning. New engineers have to be trained, and it takes them longer to make design modifications, stretching out the time required to ramp up sales yield.

Engineering management can take several steps to provide the right incentives and foster the right culture to support the learning curve. The first is to introduce an organizational measure that reflects the importance of staying focused during launch. Companies measure manufacturing success in terms of how long it takes to achieve scale production volumes, and they typically tie engineering to this metric as well. To move along the learning curve faster, though, companies need instead to focus engineering, as well as marketing and sales, on the time it takes to reach the break-even and then sustainable profitable levels of sales yield. In addition, engineers who stay involved throughout the entire learning process need to be rewarded by an assignment to another big project.

The Role of General Management

It is unlikely that incentives will be established to keep engineers involved with the product once it hits the market without the direct and daily involvement of general management. Indeed, during the first two phases, the whole management team should be focused on the customer frontier, the source of learning. CEOs and division managers must direct the efforts of those who drive the learning and participate in all crucial product and organizational decisions concerning functionality, target markets, sales channels, and marketing strategy.

Too often, executives don't get actively involved in sales strategy until a revenue gap appears and cash becomes scarce. But it is during the early stages of the learning curve that top management can have maximum impact on the ultimate outcome of the venture. Executives need to take responsibility for projecting the shape of the sales learning curve based on realistic inputs and for ensuring that all learning opportunities are identified. Then, the shape of the curve should drive the design of revenue, expense, and hiring plans across the entire organization. The longer the initiation stage, the longer the learning period and investment phase will be, and the lower the revenue expectations should be set. The most important role of all for senior executives is setting realistic expectations—guided by the curve—for investors, the board, and employees.

High-tech companies routinely "price on the learning curve"—that is, they deliberately set selling prices low on the early manufacturing runs to stimulate volume that will underwrite their efforts to gain enough experience to lower costs and ultimately reap higher profits. Like the manufacturing learning curve, the sales learning curve permits you to see all the aspects of a set of activities—in this case, the go-to-market process—through a new lens and to plan appropriately. Applying the sales learning curve as a strategic construct allows management and investors to share a common language in understanding this phase of the business. And successful management of the sales learning curve allows companies to reduce the time to profitability and the cost of breaking even, increasing the success rate of start-ups and new-category product launches.

How Big a Sales Force?

AT THE TIME OF A SUCCESSFUL BETA TEST, young companies typically carry a large fixed cost, consisting of engineering and G&A personnel. In an effort to cover those costs and become cash positive as quickly as possible, they want to ramp up sales quickly. Conventional wisdom suggests that the only way to drive sales is by hiring sales reps as early as possible. To figure out exactly how many reps to hire and when, most sales leaders use a capacity-planning model.

The basic formula for calculating the number of salespeople needed to reach the break-even cash flow point is to divide the total fixed costs by the marginal contribution of an average sales rep (revenue minus cost of goods sold minus total cost per rep). The first step is to calculate total cost per rep.

Say a software company pays its average sales rep $200,000 per year (base plus commission), and a sales rep incurs $50,000 per year in T&E expenses plus $80,000 in administrative and operating expenses. That totals $330,000 in direct costs per rep. To that must be added indirect costs (such as sales support and management personnel), which typically adds as much as 50% of the direct cost per rep, in this case $165,000. That brings the total cost per rep to $495,000 per year.

The next, and most challenging, step is to figure out what annual revenue it's reasonable to expect an average rep to produce once she's come fully up to speed— the "standard quota." To do so, most sales leaders rely on their past experience or the experience of other salespeople selling similar products. That works fine for mature products. Suppose, for instance, that our software company hires a star sales vice president from a *Fortune* 100 software firm. Based on his previous experience, he might expect a fully effective sales rep (FESR) to produce about $2.5 million in revenue per year, and so that's the figure he starts with as the standard quota.

Then to account for attrition and uneven performance among reps, he prudently reduces that figure by about 20% to $2 million in average revenue per rep. The software business has high incremental margins of around 90%, yielding an expected contribution of $1.8 million per rep. So, subtracting the total cost per rep of $495,000 from the expected yield, the sales VP arrives at a marginal contribution for an average rep of around $1.3 million per year.

Our company's fixed costs (engineering and G&A) are running around $12 million per year, so the sales head concludes that he needs about nine or ten sales reps to reach the break-even point. He'd get these reps on board as soon as possible and promise executive management that they'd reach break-even within 6 to 12 months, the typical time required to train and deploy new sales reps.

But let's say that our company is a start-up, and the sales VP, in an effort to be conservative about selling a totally new product in a new market, reduces his standard quota from $2.5 million to $1.5 million. That drops the marginal contribution per rep to $585,000. Plugging

in this lower marginal contribution would lead him to con-
clude he needs more like 21 sales reps.

The problem with applying the above methodology
to start-ups or new-category product launches, though, is
that it doesn't take into account the organization's sales
learning curve. Our start-up would be swamped if all 21
reps were hired from the outset, when the product was
still being refined, the go-to-market strategy had yet to be
settled, and revenues were coming in far more slowly
than they ever would for a mature product. Cash flow
would be strained, sending the company further into the
red and disappointing investors.

So what's the right way to approach capacity planning for a new-product launch? Start out with very low
assumptions about expected revenue per salesperson,
and increase these expectations gradually, quarter by
quarter. Anticipate that during the initiation phase, reps
will not generate enough revenue to cover their total
costs. Given that the marginal contribution per rep will
therefore be negative in this phase, hiring more people
will merely deteriorate your cash position. Only when
you see the productivity of existing reps approaching the
point where they cover their total costs should you consider expanding the sales force. Unfortunately, there's no
magic formula for predicting when that point will arrive.
But closely tracking your sales yield, and tying your planning assumptions to the different stages on the sales
learning curve, will prevent you from wasting critical
funds in the early stages.

Originally published in July–August 2006
Reprint R0607J

The Ultimately Accountable Job

Leading Today's Sales Organization

JEROME A. COLLETTI AND MARY S. FISS

Executive Summary

IN RECENT YEARS, sales leaders have had to devote considerable time and energy to establishing and maintaining disciplined processes. The thing is, many of them stop there—and they can't afford to, because the business environment has changed. Customers have gained power and gone global, channels have proliferated, more product companies are selling services, and many suppliers have begun providing a single point of contact for customers.

Such changes require today's sales leaders to fill various new roles:

Company leader. The best sales chiefs actively help formulate and execute company strategy, and they collaborate with all functions of the business to deliver value to customers.

Customer champion. Customers want C-level relationships with suppliers in order to understand product strategy, look at offerings in advance, and participate in decisions made about future products—and sales leaders are in the best position to offer that kind of contact.

Process guru. Although sales chiefs must look beyond the sales and customer processes they have honed over the past decade, they can't abandon them. The focus on process has become only more important as many organizations have begun bundling products and services to meet important customers' individual needs.

Organization architect. Good sales leaders spend a lot of time evaluating and occasionally redesigning the sales organization's structure to ensure that it supports corporate strategy. Often, this involves finding the right balance between specialized and generalized sales roles.

Course corrector. Sales leaders must watch the horizon, but they can't take their hands off the levers or forget about the dials. If they do, they might fail to respond when quick adjustments in priorities are needed.

W HEN IT COMES TO THINKING about sales leadership these days, most executives just don't get it. Chief sales officers—and even chief executive officers, who recognize that the sales organization drives topline growth—often have an incomplete notion of the CSO's job.

Sure, they understand that leading the modern sales organization takes much more than motivating and managing salespeople. In recent years, CSOs have had to devote considerable time and energy to establishing and maintaining disciplined sales processes, including everything from customer segmentation to sales staff compensation. Given the complexity of those processes, even well-run sales departments have to work hard to get them all operating smoothly. But many CSOs stop there—and they can't afford to. The heightened expectations of customers, peer executives in other functions, and the sales force itself require the head of sales to shoulder new responsibilities, ones that have changed the job almost beyond recognition from what it was 20 years ago.

In this article—which is based on our work with a wide range of sales organizations in more than 20 industries, plus more than a dozen in-depth interviews with chief sales officers, executives who manage CSOs, and sales leadership consultants—we first look at the ways in which the business environment has changed the sales chief's job. We then describe the new roles that sales leaders increasingly must play. This expanded job profile can be used as a template by those who want to excel in the position and by the CEOs responsible for hiring the best people to fill it.

New Environment

Examine the calendar of any successful chief sales officer, and you'll see how complex the job has become. (For an example, see the exhibit "A Week in the Life of Ben Bulkley" at the end of this article.) That complexity stems from the following changes, which have affected sales activities at most major companies.

Customers have gained power. It's no secret that in many industries, supply outstrips demand. Customers have more choices and more information—thanks largely to the Internet—about what they can buy and how they can buy it. The shift in power from sellers to buyers has made customers demand more of their suppliers and the buying experience.

Customers have gone global. The globalization of business has made the structure of many sales organizations (those with a regional or national focus) anachronistic. Suppliers had better be sure that their organizations mesh with their customers' global orientation and sourcing processes. "Gone are the days when we could think of this part of our business as 'North American' or that part as 'pan-European,'" says Joe Walker, president of the North American and European business units of Southfield, Michigan–based R. L. Polk, a major provider of customer data to automakers. "A corporate customer making a purchase decision in Detroit is doing so on behalf of his global organization."

Channels have proliferated. At one time, the direct sales force *was* the sales organization. Today, most companies, regardless of size, go to market through multiple channels. The sales organization may comprise not only people employed by the company—field sales, telesales, and online reps—but also those outside the company, including partners and resellers.

More product companies sell services. Whether wrapped around or embedded in products, complementary services have become a way to enhance or simply maintain a product's competitive edge. Selling these services calls for a special mind-set. "The holistic approach required to seamlessly package products and services together is very different from the traditional selling of product," explains Greg Shortell, the president and CEO of Network Engines, a provider of storage and security appliance services in Canton, Massachusetts. (Until recently, Shortell was a senior vice president of global sales and marketing for enterprise solutions at Nokia.) The reason for the difference, he says, is that "after a certain period of time, a customer stops buying your product and starts buying your strategy."

Suppliers have adopted a "one company" organizational structure. Business-to-business marketers selling products and solutions across many categories have moved away from a structure in which multiple business units sell separately to the same customer. Instead, sales resources companywide work together to sell all products to the customer through a single point of contact. In this newer model, sales specialists—focusing on, for example, product features or applications or technical requirements—typically support account managers, who are responsible for individual customers. The single corporate face makes life simpler for the customer. It also can boost sales results through cross selling and improved focus on providing integrated solutions that meet customer needs. But this approach increases sales expenses and can create confusion about accountability for results, presenting yet another challenge for the chief sales officer.

New Roles

These changes in the business environment have made running a sales organization more demanding than it's ever been. Sales will always be the ultimately accountable job. No other function bears such exposed responsibility for delivering on the numbers. These days, though, that is just the starting point. The successful CSO also needs to oversee sophisticated processes for such tasks as customer segmentation—processes that not long ago represented state-of-the-art practice but today are considered sales essentials. As if that were not enough, the CSO must take on five new distinct, but related, roles.

COMPANY LEADER

The chief sales officer must hit his targets while ensuring that the sales organization's actions—at all levels and across all channels—support the company's strategy. Striking that balance means communicating broader goals to the rank and file, so salespeople can connect their day-to-day responsibilities with the big picture; it also calls for effective collaboration with other functions. "Sales leaders can no longer think of themselves as working in a tight little box, responsible only for revenue generation and relationship management," says Peter Andruszkiewicz, the vice president for national account sales at health care provider Kaiser Permanente in Oakland, California.

Every CSO faces similar general objectives: achieving revenue growth, launching new products, acquiring customers, expanding business with current customers, improving sales productivity, and containing or reducing selling expenses. Only through strong leadership can sales chiefs make it clear how these goals can be achieved in support of corporate strategy. In fact, at least 15% of a CSO's time should be spent establishing and communicating a clear course for accomplishing the current year's business plan. "Without an articulation of the company's strategic direction to the sales force—and, incidentally, to customers and channel partners—you run the risk of less-than-optimal performance," says Network Engines' Greg Shortell. In large part, that's because disagreements about priorities arise.

For example, a multinational software company found that salespeople were consistently giving away the time of its billable professional services staff to secure new sales contracts. On the surface, this wasn't a bad idea. However, it ran against the corporate strategy of focusing on top-line growth at a time when there were few opportunities to increase profitability through cost cutting. The CSO believed that discretion (based on defined criteria) would be a simple fix to the problem. The hypothesis was that, if the concession were reserved for strategically important existing customers willing to experiment with new applications, complementary professional services might lead to substantial add-on revenue. After orienting its salespeople to this approach and indicating what criteria should be used to determine which customers should receive the concession, results did improve. New applications revenue from existing customers grew 35%, about three times the previous rate of growth.

The best sales chiefs are, along with the rest of the senior executive team, leaders of the company as a whole. They actively participate in formulating company strategy as well as executing it. No enlightened CEO considers entering a new market, expanding the company's product portfolio, or taking on a new channel without seeking the advice of the CSO—that is, if the CSO has won his respect and trust. For instance, a sales chief can offer valuable insights about the company's customers: which ones plan to grow, where their growth will come from, and what their particular needs will be. "My CEO expects that I will bring him market intelligence about what our customers require from us so they can be successful in their business," says Mary Delaney, who leads a 600-person sales force for the online job broker Career-Builder.

As an integral part of the senior executive team, sales chiefs are also expected to collaborate with all functions of the business in delivering value to customers. Indeed, they should lead the creation of an environment in which people across the organization see themselves as members of a customer-facing team.

A sales chief can take on an even higher profile role in a company where the sales function hasn't traditionally been a priority, such as in a professional services firm or a real estate investment trust. In such a case, the CSO must lead a cultural revolution, building a sales organization that promotes the firm's commitment to growth in partnership with its customers.

Consider the following example. The partners in a major regional accounting firm were concerned that their business was not growing as fast as others in the industry. After several failed attempts to spur growth through a part-time approach to sales, they decided to appoint a full-time partner in charge of sales. According to Ford Harding, president of the sales and marketing consulting firm Harding & Company, professional services firms need "a formal process to provide sales leadership both in acquiring clients and in managing the relationships in those accounts." Bringing a previously unheard-of focus and consistency to the sales process did, in fact, yield faster growth for the accounting firm. Before this investment in the sales leader role, fees grew at a rate of 5% a year. Two years after the change, fees grew more than 10% year over year, and this trend has continued. The partners believe that this is the result of the shift to a formal sales process with its own leadership, as well as improved business conditions.

CUSTOMER CHAMPION

If the customer is king these days, who lives within his inner circle? Of all the functions, the sales organization comes closest, and the CSO is thus the most effective conduit for funneling customer-related insights to the rest of the senior executive team. The successful sales leader spends more time with customers today not only because they have valuable things to say but also because they demand to be heard by their suppliers' most senior people. As other, nonsales senior executives throughout the company respond to such demands, the CSO can serve as a role model for his peers in interacting with customers.

Customers want close contact with their suppliers' senior executives in order to understand product strategy, look at new offerings in advance, and help with decisions about how future products will meet their particular needs. They also want top-level contact so they will have someone to call when something goes wrong—an inevitability in even the best of customer-supplier relationships. Through frequent conversations with its major customers, financial information provider Dun & Bradstreet learned that they wanted a link, above the account manager level, with the company's sales organization. "Our customers are looking for a C-level-to-C-level relationship that they count on as a safety net in the event that our people and their people hit an impasse as they work together," says Mike Collins, D&B's vice president for sales operations. "If issues arise, relationships are already in place."

Such a relationship clearly benefits suppliers, as well. It provides an invaluable window into a customer's growth plans—a window that otherwise might not exist. Network Engines' Greg Shortell says that most customers, regardless of the product, have a buying cycle. "During that time," he adds, "they will work with you, giving you the luxury of guiding their future. At the end of that period, if you have done your job well, you're likely to be in an advantageous position to supply their needs." The head of sales is both a natural person to establish this sort of relationship and the one best positioned to translate the needs of important customers into useful strategic information for senior executives in her company.

Of course, it isn't always easy for suppliers to forge these high-level relationships, especially since customers' purchasing managers (who are growing more sophisticated and aggressive and are charged mainly with getting the best price) may view such relationships warily. What's more, the use of the Internet to secure and filter initial bids takes some personal contact out of the process. "Squeezing the relationship out of the equation makes it very difficult to create and sustain C-level contacts," says Ron Drake, a managing director of eFunds International, which sells electronic payment and financial risk management systems to financial institutions, retailers, governments, and other organizations worldwide.

So CSOs need to find opportunities to share their business insights with senior executives at client companies as a way of keeping the conversation alive. Drake, responsible for eFunds' business in Europe, the Middle East, and Africa, says that the U.S.-based company's

global outlook gives it a foot in the door for C-level conversations: "We can talk about what other companies are
doing around the world, something senior executives are
interested in." That helps counter the trend toward a
limited sales role in the company's key industries of
banking and telecommunications, he adds.

PROCESS GURU

As we have seen, CSOs increasingly must have a dual
perspective, looking outward toward customers and
inward at their own organizations. Over the past decade,
they have honed their processes for selling products and
services and managing customer relationships. In fact, a
CSO may spend 10% to 20% of her time defining, creating, managing, and improving such processes—or sifting
through stacks of proposals from consultants and sales-
training companies offering database applications, customer relationship management tools, process maps,
and other approaches.

   This focus on process has become particularly important as many organizations have moved beyond selling
discrete products or services and toward "solutions selling," putting together bundled offerings of products and
services designed to meet important customers' individual needs. (See the sidebar "Selling to Solve" at the end of
this article.) Careful reinvention and oversight of the
sales process are critical also in the case of a merger, an
acquisition, or a new product introduction.

   Adopting a true sales leadership role may mean dele-
gating some of the process-related tasks that currently
occupy so much of a CSO's time. Directly managing
the continual upgrading of foundational processes—
customer segmentation, sales channel management,

technology support—can be a dangerous distraction from more important leadership challenges. "Best practices are a constantly moving target, and there really is no silver bullet," says Alan Cervasio, vice president for global sales strategy at Marriott Vacation Club International in Orlando, Florida. The dogged pursuit of world-class performance in these processes, while essential, can be handled by others.

ORGANIZATION ARCHITECT

A good CSO should also spend a significant amount of her time evaluating and occasionally redesigning the sales organization's structure to ensure that it supports the company's strategic goals. Often, this involves finding the right balance between specialized and generalized sales roles. In a generalist sales organization, each representative or account manager sells a company's entire, but usually limited, product line to customers who typically are all in the same industry, thus providing a single point of business contact to customers. As a supplier's product portfolio grows larger and more complex, though, or if the customers are numerous and from different industries, some sales specialization is usually required. Indeed, the broader the portfolio and the greater the number of markets in which the customers operate, the greater the need for specialization. That need can be met by a sales force of generalist sales reps supported by product sales specialists, for instance, or by separate specialty forces dedicated to a single product or market.

Many business-to-business marketers have adopted the generalists-supported-by-specialists model as their product portfolios or solution sets have broadened. The result has been a shift in the locus of sales activity from the business unit, which had separate sales and service functions, to a single companywide sales unit comprising account managers and sales specialists who cover all customers and markets. Because this approach offers customers "one-face, one bag" as they make their purchases, it has caught on with suppliers.

Given the potential for increased sales costs and confusion about accountability for results, however, it is becoming clear that some CSOs have overspecialized their organizations. A recent study of 12 technology companies—conducted by the consulting firm Growth Solutions, a business partner of ours—showed that senior management in each company was actively looking for ways to simplify the sales model, which may require dismantling or at least streamlining some of these specialized organizations. The trend toward specialization can be attributed to a combination of factors: revenue growth, product line expansion, and mergers that aren't followed with careful product line rationalization. After a merger, for example, integration team leaders often add sales specialists for the sake of politics and appeasement instead of designing sales coverage in response to a rigorous customer segmentation exercise.

Whatever the mix of generalists and specialists, it will always elicit protest. Product managers complain, "Without specialists, my product line will not receive the necessary sales support to achieve plan." Sales managers reply, "We have the relationships with the customers. If you blow up our account management organization, the value of this acquisition is going south!"

Because sales specialization is so common today in companies selling multiple product lines, the CSO needs to determine whether it costs more than the resulting sales and margins justify. He should be looking at financial measures (the cost of generating revenue growth, assessed by channel, new market segment, and new product); customer measures (account revenue retention, the number of new accounts acquired at or above a defined revenue threshold, and the proportion of business derived from new and existing customers); and sales productivity measures (quotas, the average size of sales transactions, and the balance of sales across multiple products in target accounts). A detailed assessment of the sales force's structure will need to be repeated after any number of corporate developments—for example, the introduction of a new product.

COURSE CORRECTOR

A sales chief always needs to be looking at some point on the horizon, then designing and redesigning the sales organization to help the company get there. But the CSO can't take her hands off the levers or forget about the dials, or she might fail to respond to signs that a quick adjustment in sales priorities is needed. The best CSOs will tell you that missing annual revenue and margin goals is simply not an option in their companies. Consistent, predictable performance is expected, so they have to manage their organizations for results, using short-cycle data and analysis. Investments in staff, CRM technology, and tools for account planning, forecasting, and quota allocation have made sales performance data—organized by segment, channel, and sales process—more readily available to sales executives. Of course, that information has little value unless it is put to intelligent use.

Nokia has assembled a back-office staff (what the company calls a sales operations team) that includes a sales controller and sales analysts who monitor, measure, and chart sales results. Greg Shortell says that when he was with Nokia, this team allowed him to relinquish basic navigational duties and spend more time with customers. But when alerted to a problem—he received sales performance data twice a day—he had to be ready to rapidly change course.

Salespeople in the field are sometimes reluctant to respond to requests from senior management for such detailed information. Managed properly, though, the information exchange can be very productive for both sides. "While our sales force owns the responsibility for relationships and sales results, I make it clear to them that our leadership team welcomes requests for help," says David "Skip" Prichard, president of the higher education and library unit at ProQuest, an information management company in Ann Arbor, Michigan. "At the same time, they must tell us when we are 'helping too much,' interfering in their customer relationships."

As PRICHARD'S COMMENT SUGGESTS, the pressures on a chief sales officer come from without and within, from above and below. We've laid out a daunting portfolio of roles that a sales leader must embrace if his organization is going to provide the profitable top-line growth the company expects. Over time, the job description is likely to become even more demanding. As Alan Cervasio of Marriott Vacation Club International says, "CSOs must hold the view that sales, as a function, is continuously evolving. There is no constant state, only a state in which you are clear about what you need to be changing to in order to succeed."

A Week in the Life of Ben Bulkley

An evolving business world has forced chief sales officers to take on a variety of new roles. Here's a look at how these responsibilities help shape a typical week for Ben Bulkley, who heads the worldwide sales organization at Invitrogen, a provider of life science products and services in Carlsbad, California.

Monday	AM	· Monthly global business review, North America (conference call)
	PM	· Company Pricing Council meeting
		· Sales Force Effectiveness Project update
		· eBusiness update
		· Monthly global business review, Asia-Pacific (evening conference call because of time difference)
Tuesday	AM	· Product business unit marketing meeting
	PM	· Preparation for next week's industry association board meeting and company analyst meeting
		· Flight to London
Wednesday	AM	· Meetings with Customer X (outside London):
		General discussion with top executives about customer's business strategy
		Workshop on latest developments in intellectual property protection

As a **process guru,** Bulkley ensures that sales process changes are integrated into daily sales activities.

As an **organization architect,** he determines whether the online ordering system may require a redesign of direct sales strategies.

As a **customer champion,** he strengthens the company's C-level relationship with the customer by providing information about the latest developments on industry issues (rather than merely giving product information).

	PM	• Meetings with Customer X:
		    Tour of company manufacturing plant
		• Flight to Glasgow
		• Dinner with European field office staff;
		    discussion of particular customer challenges

Thursday	AM	• Flight to Paris • Meetings with Customer Y (outside Paris): General discussion with top executives about customer's business strategy
	PM	• Meetings with Customer Y: Workshop on latest trends in U.S. National Institutes of Health research funding • Flight to Los Angeles
Friday	AM	• Sales manager's leadership development workshop • One-on-one coaching of high-potential sales manager • Interview job candidates for top sales positions
	PM	• Review detailed weekly sales update by region and product • Cross-functional meeting on new business development initiatives • Review Customer Z account plan with executives from product development and customer service in preparation for next week's meeting with Customer Z (Shanghai)
Saturday	AM	• Strategic-planning meeting with project team in preparation for Monday's presentation to CEO and rest of executive management team

As a **course corrector**, he watches for subtle signs that sales strategy needs to be retooled.

As a **company leader**, he collaborates with other functions to align product development and sales strategies.

Selling to Solve

IT'S THE BYWORD OF MODERN MARKETING: Instead of selling simple products or services, companies sell "solutions." That presents particular challenges for sales leaders to manage. Instead of simply getting a customer to choose their products over rivals', they draw on an array of corporate and external capabilities to design an integrated offering meant to solve a customer-specific problem.

Companies view solutions selling as a way to build strong relationships with customers and earn price premiums for the value they deliver. Because it can be incredibly inefficient and expensive, however, suppliers must identify their most strategic customers and offer solutions packages only to them. Even after doing this, suppliers may learn that some of those customers aren't interested in making the investment on their end. Customers might want to do things the old way, simply completing a transaction to buy a product or service.

Too often, companies commit to solutions selling without completely understanding what they need to be successful. The sales chief considering this approach not only must understand the process but also must structure the organization to support it. That includes having the competencies—somewhere in the organization, if not in sales—to negotiate with external partners who will be needed to help craft solutions. It also means that the field organization must be trained in solutions selling. Whereas the traditional sales relationship involves a series of transactions, selling solutions calls for a consultative relationship in which those who do the selling add value. Finally, the CSO needs to confirm that the delivery

organization has been trained in solutions implementa-
tion, since the customer is going to hold the supplier
accountable for a single point of delivery.

If the solutions-selling processes—from start to finish—
are not right, then profit margins are likely to suffer
because of redos or givebacks such as partial refunds or
future concessions.

Originally published in July–August 2006
Reprint R0607K

About the Contributors

ERIN ANDERSON is the John H. Loudon Chaired Professor of International Management at Insead in Fontainebleau, France, and the director of Leading the Effective Sales Force, a joint program of Insead and the Wharton School in Philadelphia.

DAVID CHAMPION is senior editor of *Harvard Business Review*.

JEROME A. COLLETTI is the managing partner at Colletti-Fiss, a Scottsdale, Arizona–based management consulting firm specializing in sales effectiveness.

JIM DICKIE is a partner at CSO Insights, a San Francisco–based research firm that studies how companies market, sell, and provide service to customers.

MARY S. FISS is a partner at Colletti-Fiss, a Scottsdale, Arizona–based management consulting firm specializing in sales effectiveness.

DAVID GODES is an associate professor at Harvard Business School in Boston.

FRED HASSAN is the CEO of Schering-Plough.

CHARLES A. HOLLOWAY is the Kleiner Perkins Caufield & Byers Professor of Management, Emeritus at Stanford Graduate School of Business in California.

PHILIP KOTLER is the S.C. Johnson & Son Distinguished Professor of International Marketing at Northwestern University's Kellogg School of Management in Evanston, Illinois.

SUJ KRISHNASWAMY is the founder and principal of Stinsights, a Chicago-based business strategy and market research firm specializing in sales-marketing interface.

MARK LESLIE is the managing director of the private investment company Leslie Ventures, a lecturer at Stanford Graduate School of Business and Stanford's Graduate School of Engineering, and the retired founder, chairman, and CEO of Veritas Software.

SALLY E. LORIMER is a marketing and sales consultant and a business writer based in Northville, Michigan.

VINCENT ONYEMAH is an assistant professor of marketing at Boston University's School of Management.

NEIL RACKHAM is a visiting professor at the University of Portsmouth in England.

PRABHAKANT SINHA is a cochairman of ZS Associates.

THOMAS A. STEWART is editor and managing director of *Harvard Business Review*.

BARRY TRAILER is a partner at CSO Insights, a San Francisco–based research firm that studies how companies market, sell, and provide service to customers.

TUBA ÜSTÜNER is a lecturer at Cass Business School in London.

ANDRIS A. ZOLTNERS is a professor of marketing at Northwestern University's Kellogg School of Management in Evanston, Illinois.

Index